1920S BRITAIN

Janet Shepherd & John Shepherd

SHIRE LIVING HISTORIES

How we worked • How we played • How we lived

Published in Great Britain in 2010 by Shire Publications Ltd,
Midland House, West Way, Botley, Oxford OX2 0PH,
United Kingdom.
44-02 23rd Street, Suite 219, Long Island City, NY 11101,
USA.

E-mail: shire@shirebooks.co.uk   www.shirebooks.co.uk

© 2010 Shire Publications.

Every attempt has been made by the Publishers to secure
the appropriate permissions for materials reproduced in
this book. If there has been any oversight we will be happy
to rectify the situation and a written submission should be
made to the Publishers.

A CIP catalogue record for this book is available from the
British Library.

Shire Living Histories no. 5. ISBN-13: 978 0 74780 792 6

Janet and John Shepherd have asserted their right under
the Copyright, Designs and Patents Act, 1988, to be
identified as the authors of this book.

Designed by Myriam Bell Design, France and typeset in
Perpetua, Jenson Text and Gill Sans.

Printed in China through Worldprint Ltd.

10 11 12 13 14   10 9 8 7 6 5 4 3 2 1

COVER IMAGE
Picadilly, 1926. Painting for London, Midland & Scottish
Railway poster, by Maurice Greiffenhagen. (Science &
Society Picture Library)

PHOTOGRAPH ACKNOWLEDGEMENTS

Authors' collection, pages 8 (bottom), 11 (left and right),
17, 24 (bottom), 42; Bancroft Road Library, pages 9 (top
and bottom), 14 (top and bottom), 15 (bottom), 20, 32,
33, 34, 35, 39, 40 (top), 48, 49 (top), 58, 72 (top), 73,
75; Brenda Corn, page 40; Cambridgeshire Collection,
Central Library, Cambridge, pages 56 (left), 74; Getty
Images, pages 6, 8 (top), 12, 15 (top), 16, 18 (top and
bottom), 22 (bottom), 26, 27 (bottom), 28, 46 (top), 55
(bottom), 57, 59, 66, 67, 70, 72 (bottom), 83, 84, 85;
Ivy Elliott, page 30; Jenny Childs, page 22 (top); Les
Waters, pages 25, 49 (bottom), 51, 80 (top); Mary
Simpson, page 24 (top); Pat Perry, page 31; Ray Collier,
page 46 (bottom); Robert Opie Collection, pages 4, 10,
19, 27 (top), 36, 41, 44, 47, 50, 52, 54, 55 (top), 56
(right), 62, 64 (left and right), 65, 78, 80 (bottom), 81,
82; Robin Barraclough, page 23; Sandra Lee, page 76;
Shire Publications, pages 60–1; Sue Woodhouse, page 68;
West Yorkshire Archives Service, Leeds, pages 38, 43.

AUTHORS' ACKNOWLEDGEMENTS

We are most grateful to the following for providing
photographs: Patrick Chaplin, Jenny Childs, Ray Collier,
Brenda Corn, Ivy Elliott, Kevin Knight, Keith Laybourn,
Sandra Lee, Pat Perry, Mary Simpson, Les Waters, Sue
Woodhouse.

Chris Lloyd, archivist, Bancroft Road Library;
Cambridgeshire Collection, Central Library Cambridge;
Getty Archives; Robert Opie Collection, West Yorkshire
Archives (Leeds).

Also, thanks to many family and friends, especially in Dry
Drayton, who assisted, or lent photos which, for reasons
of space, could not be included.

A very special word of thanks to Bev Harding and Les
Waters, for invaluable technical assistance and advice.

Shire Publications is supporting the Woodland Trust, the UK's leading woodland conservation charity, by funding the dedication of trees.

CONTENTS

OFFICIAL DAILY PROGRAMME

3D

BRITISH EMPIRE
EXHIBITION
1924

FRIDAY

PREFACE

FOLLOWING the shocking trauma of the First World War, the attempt to return to anything like normality was bound to be difficult. Not only had the personal suffering been so painful and widespread, but when the surviving soldiers returned home they discovered that the war had brought such deep social and economic change that familiar old ways of life had changed forever. As a result, the 1920s were, not surprisingly, a time of dramatic contrasts, a time when in some ways the transformation of the country continued apace, while in others people grimly tried to revert to familiar old ways. In some respects there was a rush towards a youthful modernity, to an escape from the constraints of the Victorian age through new technologies, mass media and mass travel. In others, traditional institutions such as the Church survived unscathed. Politically, old class tensions were worked out in distinctively British ways, as the country instinctively recoiled from the example of the Russian revolution and its aftermath, and opted for stability where it mattered.

In this book, Janet Shepherd and John Shepherd explore the history of these years, balancing an overview of life with the distinct, and diverse examples of the individual experiences of their own parents. They explore what it meant to live in the metropolis of an empire at its greatest geographical extent, at a time when Britain's towns and cities were sprawling out into the countryside, and where the cinema brought dreams of glamorous ways of living to every high street.

Peter Furtado
General Editor

Opposite:
An 'Official Daily Programme' for Friday's entrance to the British Empire Exhibition at Wembley in 1924, showing The India Pavilion and the lake. Admission for an adult was one shilling and sixpence. In 1924, the British Empire encompassed a quarter of the world's land surface, with possessions in fifty-eight countries. The exhibition was the first occasion on which the Post Office issued commemorative stamps.

5

INTRODUCTION: TOTAL WAR TO WALL STREET CRASH

A S THE GUNS fell silent at the end of the Great War, the British Prime Minister, David Lloyd George, famously promised to make Britain a 'fit country for heroes to live in'. Instead, disenchanted ex-servicemen, returning home from the trauma and carnage of the Western Front, found only mass unemployment, high prices, poor housing and widespread poverty. The post-war mood of despondency and despair deepened. Spanish influenza killed around a quarter of a million in Britain and forty million worldwide, far more than wartime casualties.

Many of the enduring images of the 1920s present a grim picture of British life in a class-conscious and class-divided society. 'Dole queues' of the unemployed, desperate for meagre government assistance, were a familiar scene. In 1921, thirty Poplar Labour councillors spent six weeks in prison in a struggle to defend their local poor and destitute east London community. The industrial crisis, resulting in the General Strike of 1926, split the nation and brought Britain to a standstill for nine days with armoured vehicles on London streets. In the inter-war years, hunger marches of jobless men from the Welsh valleys, industrial north and Scotland aroused hostility as well as sympathy. Finally, the 'Wall Street Crash' of October–November 1929 in America ushered in a world depression that did not end until another international conflict began in 1939.

Yet, 1920s Britain is also remembered as the 'Roaring Twenties' – for the 'flappers', 'Bright Young Things', Art Deco, new crazes such as jazz and the Charleston, as well as Howard Carter's discovery of Tutankhamun's magnificent tomb and Rudolph Valentino on the silver screen. The 1920s saw new suburban houses, some with a motor car parked outside, and arterial roads with modern industrial developments. Listening to the wireless, going to the pictures, FA Cup finals at Wembley and filling in the new weekly football pools at home – all became part of British popular culture.

Opposite:
Joan Crawford and Johnny Mack Brown dance the Charleston in the silent American MGM film *Our Dancing Daughters* in 1928. The Charleston was 'all the rage' among the younger generation when it arrived in Britain from America in 1925.

7

Imperial Britain remained a major world power at the heart of a global economy. The British premier's peacemaking in Paris with the president of the United States, and the prime ministers of France and Italy, symbolised this country's world pre-eminence.

In these post-war years, the clarion call of British politicians and businessmen was for 'a return to normalcy'. British economic and political eminence had been built on almost a century and a half of industrial growth and British dominance in world markets. However in the 1920s, the prospect of a new dawn in a world shattered by economic collapse, enflamed by the Bolshevik Revolution and teetering on the brink of international conflict, seemingly proved illusory.

In 1918, the Representation of the People Act extended the vote to all adult males over twenty-one and women over thirty. Ramsay MacDonald, a fifty-seven-year-old Scottish widower, who had inspired thousands by his charismatic socialist oratory and vision of Jerusalem in Britain's green and pleasant land, in 1924 became Britain's first Labour prime minister and also foreign secretary. Ishbel, his twenty-year-old daughter and political hostess at 10 Downing Street, had to go to the local Co-op sales to purchase furniture and household effects, traditionally provided by former wealthy Liberal and Conservative prime ministers. The middle and upper classes in the 1920s still dominated the professions, business and British politics. MacDonald surprisingly recruited Conservatives, Liberals and a former Viceroy of India for his first Cabinet, as well as the predictable Labour party and trade union figures. Yet, for the first time, it was a government more representative of the British nation.

But for ordinary working families Imperial Britain in the 1920s was often a nation of empty promises and lost opportunities. British

At Westminster: Nancy Astor (Con) and Margaret Wintringham (Lib), first and second women MPs to take their seats in Parliament, 1921. Women remained grossly under-represented in Parliament and those under the age of thirty did not gain the vote until 1928.

Lest we forget: The Cenotaph, Whitehall, 1920s. This permanent national memorial to the fallen sailors, soldiers and airmen of the First World War was erected in 1920. By 1922, almost every town and city had a war memorial to remember the dead.

CENOTAPH AND WHITEHALL, LONDON.   209370.JV

Some of the poorest workers in London's East End: two Poplar dustmen with horse and cart, 1920s.

class divisions and distinctions between rich and poor were visible in widely varying life chances and in marked differences in health, education, working and living conditions.

In the 1920s, despite limited welfare legislation pioneered by the Liberal governments of 1905–14, Britain had no modern welfare state, nor a universal free national health service, which was only introduced after 1945. Those who could not afford private provision had no guaranteed basic income, no safety net against sickness, old age or unemployment. Instead, there was only traditional charitable assistance from various agencies or recourse to the pawnbroker or moneylender, at extortionate interest rates. The dreaded Poor Law and workhouse system continued to cast a long dark shadow over inadequate social provision until the Second World War.

In inter-war Britain, the quality of housing varied markedly, dependent upon social class and income. In expanding city suburbs, builders and developers produced a property boom; houses were for sale to professional people and skilled artisans. The growth of London was reflected in the development of the new outer suburbs, especially 'Metro-Land' whose residents commuted on the Metropolitan underground line to their London offices. For manual and unskilled workers, council housing for rent first became available in the 1920s. Yet slums and

The Poplar Rates Rebellion of 1921: 'some of the people for whom the council fought'. Women and children in the poor East End constituency of Poplar. George Lansbury and twenty-nine Poplar Labour councillors spent six weeks in prison defying central government by refusing to levy precept rates on their poor east London community.

An advert for Shell Motor Oil aimed at the more affluent private motorist.

run-down homes in both urban and rural areas remained a major social problem.

Transport expanded in British cities, particularly with an increase in the number of cars, buses and, in London, the development of an extended underground network. In 1924, thousands of visitors flocked to the British Empire Exhibition in the new London suburb of Wembley. The year before, two hundred thousand, twice the expected number, had travelled by underground hoping to see the first FA Cup final between Bolton Wanderers and West Ham United at the new venue. Other new forms of public transport included electronic trolley buses, although trams survived until after the Second World War. Car ownership trebled between 1920 and 1929, with many middle-class families purchasing a new British-built Austin or Morris. During this time, London remained a world city of over seven million inhabitants, the seat of government and home of monarchy. The metropolis was an international port at the heart of the British Empire, comprising different communities and traditions. However, as Charles Booth's monumental study, *Life and Labour of the People in London*, had already revealed by the turn of the century, London was a capital city of great inequalities, with extremes of wealth and poverty. During the 1920s the level of infant mortality decreased as the virulence of killer diseases lessened. However, health prospects and life chances of infants depended on class and social geography. In London, babies in working-class Shoreditch in the deprived East End were twice as likely to die in their first year than those in well-heeled Hampstead in the north, or middle-class Lewisham, south of the river.

The 1920s was also a significant decade for women in British society and politics. Many women had replaced conscripted men in certain jobs during the war, but only a minority remained employed afterwards. For the younger generation of mainly upper-middle-class women, often dubbed the 'flappers', the war brought social freedoms to be pursued and enjoyed with new lifestyles in the 1920s.

While in 1928, as Britain finally edged towards a mass political democracy, all women aged over twenty-one gained the parliamentary franchise, they remained demonstrably under-represented in parliament and in government. The 1920s was a decade of 'firsts' for women in politics. In 1920, Conservative Lady Astor became the first woman MP to take her seat in the House of Commons; by 1924, Margaret Bondfield, Labour, was the first to become a government minister. Five years on, in 1929, Ramsay MacDonald appointed Bondfield as the first woman Cabinet minister in his second Labour government.

However, during this decade, the campaign for birth control, particularly for working women, became a far more significant political and social issue than women's suffrage.

The story of 1920s Britain is that of a nation experiencing stability and change in work and play. All four of the authors' parents lived through the 1920s, experiencing the struggle, hardships and joys of rising expectations in post-war Britain. Ernest Seeley and Queenie Powell were born in 1900 in London, and in 1908 in South Wales respectively. Both went to grammar school, were the first from their working-class families to benefit from higher education, and became university and school teachers. Sam Shepherd and Violet (Vi) Chapman were born in 1913, and 1912, in east and north London respectively. After elementary school, they went straight into work in manual occupations. Our parents, and thousands of their generation, resided, worked and played in the conurbation of Greater London, still a world city of national and international standing and significance.

Below left: Ernest Seeley, standing, with younger brothers, Albert and Stanley (right), Islington, north London, mid-1920s. Ernest was a college lecturer, Albert a civil servant. Stanley's occupation at this time is unknown. Each brother is wearing a collar and tie but only Ernest has the old-fashioned stiff formal collage. All were Labour voters yet note the portrait on the wall of the Victorian Liberal Prime Minister, William Gladstone.

Below: Queenie Powell on a day out, 1929.

WORK

DURING THE 1920s, Britain remained a global power and trading nation with a vast overseas empire and colonies. After a century and a half of industrialisation, the nation's economic pre-eminence was based on manufacturing power and financial services. British people, manufactures, finance and technology had dominated the world. Despite a short-lived post-war boom until mid-1920, Britain's main staple industries – coal, textiles, iron and steel and shipbuilding – were in serious decline. The older industrial regions of Yorkshire, Lancashire, South Wales and Scotland suffered high concentrations of mass unemployment and widespread poverty.

Yet, there was a different side to life in Britain, especially in London's growing suburbs, the south and the Midlands. The rise of 'new' industries, particularly electrical goods, chemicals and motor vehicles, accompanied by a revolution in communications and an expansion in council housing and speculative house building, aided economic recovery in the inter-war years.

In world trade, Britain faced competition from America, Germany and Japan. Her share of international commerce inevitably diminished as other countries industrialised. British coal, the bedrock of Britain's industrial revolution, kept fires and furnaces burning at home. Exports of a hundred million tons a year by 1913, however, fell by a third after the war. Out-of-date British coal mines were less efficient compared to their counterparts in France, Germany, Poland and Belgium.

Lancashire textile mills had once supplied the world, but now faced severe competition in overseas markets from Indian and Japanese cotton firms equipped with modern machinery. British shipyards had expanded to meet wartime demands. In the post-war years, substantial orders were lost to America and Japan, as well as to Holland, Norway and Sweden.

By 1920, eight hundred thousand men, including coal miners, workers in textiles, engineering and shipyard workers, were jobless

Opposite:
Forgotten soldier: an unemployed ex-serviceman with no pension and 'wife and children to support' tries to earn money with his performing dog in busy Camden Town, north London, 1929. Note the advertisement behind him for a performance of Charles Dickens' 'best loved story', *David Copperfield*, at The Empire Theatre.

and reliant on minimal government assistance or charity. The 1920 Unemployment Insurance Act extended the six months' provision of unemployment benefits – 'the dole' introduced in 1911 – to nearly twelve million 'insured' workers earning less than £250 per year. An unemployed man received fifteen shillings a week (around a third of what a job seeker in twenty-first-century Britain might receive per week), a woman twelve shillings, for fifteen weeks in any one year. This wholly inadequate measure, designed initially for ex-servicemen temporarily out of work, did not cover agricultural labourers or domestic servants. Those who had not been contributing to the state scheme received nothing. In 1921, men who had exhausted their benefits could apply to the local Poor Law Guardians for 'the dole'.

Above:
William Thomas, coalman, with a coal merchant's truck at Cade's Coal Depot, Mile End, 1928. The collapse of the coal industry after the First World War also affected local coal suppliers.

The British Medical Association calculated a family with three children needed twenty-two shillings for food for one week alone (not counting fuel, clothing and other household expenditure) when the maximum benefit for a man was only thirty shillings.

In 1921, one of the worst years of the economic depression fast spreading across different regions of Britain, the Ministry of Transport constructed the North Circular Road, around outer London from Woodford to Ealing, as part of an unemployment relief scheme.

Right:
The *Milverton* (broken up in 1925) in dock dominates Manchester Road, Cubitt Town, in London's East End. This striking and rare photograph, *c.* 1920 shows the close proximity of the docks to local housing. A workman repairs rigging on a mast high above the street. Below him are an old-style motor bus with an uncovered top, a traditional horse and cart, a lorry, a pedal cycle and several pedestrians.

The first of the famous hunger marches in inter-war Britain, organised by Wal Hannington's National Unemployed Workers Movement, took place in June 1921, from London to the Labour Party Conference at Brighton.

In the same year, in one of the poorest areas of east London, the socialist George Lansbury led Labour councillors, including his son and daughter-in-law, in the 'Poplar Rates Revolt' – an extended struggle with the central authorities over an unfair rating system. The councillors, comprising twenty-five men and five women – including Cllr Nellie Cressall who was heavily pregnant – willingly went to Brixton and Holloway prisons to defend unemployed and destitute constituents.

British trade unions had emerged stronger after the war in terms of organisation and finances. Membership peaked in 1920 at over eight million but with the onset of the depression numbers fell by around thirty-five per cent. Enforced wage cuts and high levels of joblessness raised class tensions and industrial action, culminating in the 1926 General Strike organised by the TUC to support Britain's locked-out miners.

Above:
Wal Hannington, organiser of the National Unemployed Workers Movement, addresses jobless workers in Trafalgar Square, 1921. Hannington led the first, rarely mentioned, hunger march from London to Brighton in June 1921. George Lansbury addressed the marchers who then spoke to the Labour party conference in the Brighton Dome.

Left:
Crowds watch a large food convoy during the General Strike, 1926, moving from London's East End towards the City, protected by armed soldiers.

Significant pockets of rural poverty and unemployment also could not be ignored. In Cambridgeshire, farm wages were about ten shillings a week in the 1890s, and increased steadily to two pounds in the years before the First World War, but fell back in the 1920s recession and again during the 1926 General Strike. Though the overall workforce expanded during the inter-war years, from nearly sixteen million to over nineteen million, large numbers of men, women and young apprentices remained out of work, often for long periods of time. Incredibly, *The Golden Comic*, produced for children in the 1920s, found humour in two characters called Daniel Dole and Oscar Out of Work.

During the First World War, particularly after the introduction of military conscription in 1916, women had gradually taken over certain jobs traditionally occupied by men, in munitions, industry, agriculture, government, commerce and clerical work – albeit not to the extent and as rapidly as is often believed. However, these changes proved largely temporary. There were few examples of permanent differences in women's employment, except for work in offices, banks and shops, and patterns of women's working assumed pre-war trends.

Women returned to 'home and domesticity' or were employed in unskilled occupations. Only a very reduced number resumed domestic service. Jean Rennie, born in 1906, the daughter of a Clydeside riveter, recalled her life of menial jobs in the 1920s in *Every Other Sunday*. Jean left school after achieving a Higher Leaving Certificate with honours.

A woman tries on a pair of shoes in a well-stocked shoe shop, 1920.

Sam Shepherd (left) and his younger brother Ted. Both were lorry drivers for British Drug Houses (BDH, later Glaxo) for fifty years.

Her father's unemployment meant her scholarship to Glasgow University was abandoned for work in a worsted mill.

As London expanded in the 1920s, its citizens could probably find work more easily than those in other regions. Vi Chapman attended an elementary school in Islington, but was frequently absent on Fridays. Her mother, despite calls from the school attendance officer, kept Vi and her sister, May – but not their brothers – at home for housework. At fourteen, Vi was employed at a small local Quaker printing firm, where work started after morning prayers. The firm closed for two weeks' annual unpaid holiday, although Vi was still expected to pay her mother for her 'keep'.

Sam Shepherd had also left elementary school in east London at fourteen – to work as a messenger boy, sometimes queuing at Wimbledon for a client's tickets. His brother Ted also ran messages and memorably shook hands with David Lloyd George at the National Liberal Club. Both brothers then drove lorries for British Drug Houses for fifty years, delivering pharmaceuticals to different parts of Britain, witnessing the depression in the Welsh mining valleys at first hand. Queenie Powell, from Merthyr Tydfil, left South Wales for a teaching career in London. By 1926, Ernest Seeley was a Further Education lecturer. Despite being a staunch Labour Party member, he was so worried about the national situation he drove a 'pirate' bus in the General Strike.

During the 1920s London was not only the capital of Britain, but also a major manufacturing and commercial centre, with mainly small

firms, workshops and city offices. Raw materials from the Empire flowed into Britain through the extensive London docks to the east of the metropolis.

London dominated the south-east as its developing suburbs extended into the countryside, and an extensive tube network, plus expanding bus routes, transported commuters into the City and West End for work and leisure. Britain's new diversified industries, based on consumer products mainly for the home market such as radios, household goods and food processing, created increased employment. New materials, such as rayon and nylon, made women's dresses, stockings and lingerie more affordable. Increases in real earnings and the advent of hire purchase led to rising living standards.

In the inter-war years, William Morris became Britain's largest, wealthiest, car manufacturer. His small-time business rapidly grew into a modern industrial corporation, producing twenty-thousand cars in 1923. Similarly, Coventry became Britain's fastest-growing city, its economy based on cycle manufacturing and

Above: Workers stack bags of imported cocoa beans at Cadbury's chocolate manufacturing plant, Bournville, Birmingham, 1920. Produce from all over the British Empire flooded into Britain in the 1920s.

Right: Cars on the assembly line at the Austin factory in Birmingham. The inter-war period saw a huge boost in car production and ownership. By the late 1920s hand-built cars were declining in number, overtaken by mechanised production.

then car production, with famous British firms including Humber, Singer and Rover Cars, aviation and electrical goods. Out-of-work coal miners relocated from South Wales and the northern and industrial regions to find work in expanding Midland cities, such as Coventry.

During the 1920s, the British economy was a mixture of growth and decline. The population increased by two million, the greater proportion of whom were women. Work in retail industries contributed to rising living standards while Lancashire textile firms faced structural unemployment and shut down. Courtaulds, ICI, Ford and Austin became well-known firms in the new diversified economy producing goods for the home market. Overall, earnings increased by thirty per cent.

Britain in the 1920s was a country where many families in the old industrial heartlands suffered hardship through loss of regular work, often over succeeding generations. For those in work, the standard of living rose by around thirty-five per cent. Relative affluence in inter-war Britain became associated with suburbia – arterial roads, semi-detached houses, consumer goods, giant cinemas, dance halls and spectator sports.

A Clevenit hosiery advertisement, 1920s, aimed at the growing post-war consumer market, advertising stockings 'specially dyed to give a brilliant lustre'. Women's hosiery was either made from real silk or, increasingly, from 'artificial silk' (rayon), one of the products of the new chemical industries.

TRAVEL AND TRANSPORT

THE TWENTIES WITNESSED 'a transport revolution' in Britain. Old and new forms of transportation competed for increasingly crowded space in major cities and towns. Rare film footage of 1920s Bristol shows new covered buses, motor cars, lorries, motorcycles, trams, delivery vans, as well as traditional horses and carts, and street vendors on bicycles – all controlled by one white-gloved policeman.

The rapid rise of the motor car, the development of the motor bus and, in the capital, the extension of London's unique underground 'tube' network for up to 10 miles from the city centre, were significant transport developments.

Initially, only the wealthy could afford cars but by the mid-1920s prices had dropped considerably and a small car could be purchased for £200–300. Among the professional classes, doctors, solicitors, dentists and architects – mainly men – began to acquire their own transport.

Car ownership was the ultimate goal for the aspiring middle classes, especially for recreation. Day-trips, weekends away and seaside holidays – all became possible by car. *The Illustrated London News* advertised vehicles with fold-back hoods and boots that doubled as 'luncheon drawers' for picnics.

Popular beach destinations included Torquay's sub-tropical gardens and, for Londoners, Southend, with the world's longest pier. Different resorts attracted different clienteles. Frinton and Hove targeted the middle classes, Brighton and Blackpool sought the newly mobile working class who had days out in large groups, travelling in hired multi-seater 'charabancs'.

There was a rise in car production during the 1920s as British firms emulated Ford's success in America. Most cars were hand built, including the popular mass-produced Austin Seven and 'bullnose' Morris, but by the end of the decade production was increasingly mechanised. In 1929, Ernest Seeley bought his first Austin, driving it at weekends to visit relatives in Eastbourne.

Opposite:
An early forty-four-seater Straker-Squire double-decker bus operated by Empress Motors on the route from Old Ford to Bethnal Green in March 1923. Note the solid tyres and the double advertisement for the established London firm of licensed caterers, Levy & Franks.

Charabanc outing to Gough's Caves, Cheddar, 1920s. Charabancs or 'char-a-bancs' ('carriages with wooden benches') originated in France and were long vehicles that could hold many people. They were very popular in the 1920s for sightseeing or 'works' outings, particularly to the seaside, for those who could not afford their own transport.

This was the height of luxurious, expensive British cars – the Rolls-Royce Phantom, Vauxhall 30-98, and Bentley – made for a small number of very wealthy clients.

Annual driving licences and car number plates were required under the 1903 Motor Car Act but driving tests did not become compulsory until the 1930s. Many car owners drove too fast, ignoring the 20 mph speed limit. By 1920, there were two hundred thousand cars on British roads. London congestion became a major problem. In 1924, with about fifty thousand cars passing Hyde Park Corner daily, the House of Lords debated pedestrians' vulnerability. Between 1926 and 1928, roundabouts and automatic traffic lights were installed in London, the first lights being placed at Piccadilly Circus in August

Car lunch party, Brooklands Race Track, Easter Monday, 1923. Car excursions and *al fresco* picnics became extremely popular with the increase in car ownership. After extensive refurbishment, Brooklands Motor Racing Track reopened in 1920. By 1926, the racetrack was hosting Grand Prix events.

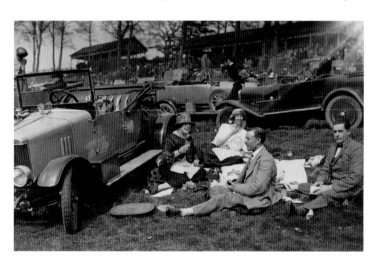

1926. Across the country, road signs were standardised. Motorists were annoyed by these new restrictions but by 1927 there were on average fourteen deaths each day on British roads.

The vast majority in Britain were unable to afford motor cars. Some purchased motorcycles that were cheaper to buy, tax and run. Many new owners, like Sam Shepherd, who bought his motorbikes in the inter-war years on hire purchase, did their own repairs in the streets outside their homes. Sidecars provided space for passengers. Moreover, a motorcycle permit could be obtained from the age of fourteen, whereas it was sixteen for a car licence.

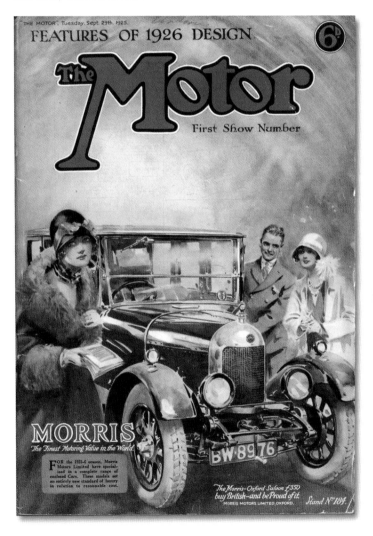

In September 1925, *The Motor* magazine featured the new Morris-Oxford saloon for £350. Note the patriotic slogan – 'Buy British and be Proud of it'.

Between the wars, pedal cycles became a popular means of transport, as well as providing independence and recreation for many. Second-hand bikes could be bought in local shops and markets and were simple to maintain. Queenie Powell used her bicycle frequently to ride into the country with college friends.

While the wealthy had a car in the garage, poorer travellers had to rely on different public services – trams, trolley buses, motor buses, steam railway and in the capital, the Underground.

By 1914, London had a large electrified tram network, but expansion had halted during the war. Afterwards, with the decline in investment, trams, with their network of cables and rails, were more expensive to modernise and maintain than the new motorised buses.

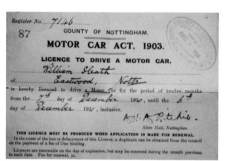

In London and in other major towns, the tram faced the challenge of the new electric trolley bus. Despite needing an overhead power supply, trolleys ran on wheels meaning there were no costly rail tracks to repair. Trams retained some popularity with their covered upper decks, seating for eighty and special offers. On weekdays in the early 1920s a reduced fare of '2d all the way' operated in central London between 10 a.m. and 4 p.m. However, gradually unable to compete with the buses, trams finally disappeared in the 1950s. Trolley buses remained in operation until diesel buses were introduced after 1945.

The 1920s witnessed the rapid growth of motor buses in most British cities. In 1923, buses carried more London passengers than

Top: Driving licence belonging to William Sleath, Nottingham, 1920–1. Annual driving licences were compulsory from 1903. Until 1930, when the design was standardised, each local authority could produce its own design and outer colour but the format was broadly similar.

Bottom: Londoners Vi Chapman and Sam Shepherd with their Ariel motorbike in the Lake District, inter-war years. Ariel was a Midlands firm based at Bournbrook, Birmingham. Ariel built very popular motorbikes in the inter-war years.

the trams for the first time. The capital's major bus company was the London General Omnibus Company (LGOC). In 1920, typical bright red 'General' buses, covered in advertisements, had uncovered rear staircases, open tops, hard tyres and cranking handles, essential before the invention of the starter button.

No routes were licensed until 1930 so independent firms were set up by anyone with sufficient resources, including a few returning military officers with gratuities. The LGOC was soon under fierce competition. It was a cut-throat affair; independent 'pirate' buses would overtake at speed, cut in, and generally attempt to outmanoeuvre the 'Generals'. These practices were eventually restricted in 1924, when a transport strike led to The London Traffic Act which introduced new regulations for London's traffic.

Two girls with bikes, Cambridge, 1920s. Cycling provided an extremely popular and cheap means of transport and recreation in the inter-war years. The Raleigh Bicycle Company, based in Nottingham, one of the oldest bicycle companies in the world, was Britain's leading cycle firm in the 1920s.

No roofs were permitted in the early 1920s, in case buses toppled over, so top-deck passengers had to tolerate all weathers. Otherwise, however, bus design was not standardised until the end of the decade when buses were enclosed, pneumatic tyres made rides smoother and engine improvements meant there were fewer breakdowns.

Prior to 1914, bus companies mainly employed men as drivers, conductors, inspectors and office workers. Women took over many of these jobs during the war, but afterwards, a male workforce again predominated. Bus employment was seen as respectable and secure. The uniforms gave a sense of identity and there was no need to buy work clothes.

Suburban developments fuelled the growth of bus routes. By 1929, many reached outer London, going into the 'metro-land' of Hertfordshire, Middlesex and Buckinghamshire and also into Essex, Kent, Surrey and Berkshire. New 'Greyhound' buses carried passengers between cities, such as the London to Bristol line that began in 1925. Before he bought his Austin, Ernest Seeley, a keen rambler, would regularly travel by bus out into the Hertfordshire countryside.

The London buses' major competition was the 'tube' – the first underground system in the world and the first to operate electric trains. The extension of tube lines to the suburbs was the major

London tram driven by a volunteer driver during the 1926 General Strike. A skeleton staff of non-unionised workers and students (Ernest Seeley drove a bus) controversially kept London's buses, trams, trains and delivery vans running. The TUC organised the General Strike – 'the most important industrial conflict in British history' – to support the miners locked out by coal owners trying to enforce reductions in wages and conditions.

development of the 1920s, enabling residents to commute to the City, avoiding the increasing road congestion. A 1924 *Evening Standard* advertisement described trains on the new Moorgate to Hampstead line as not only 'the most luxurious in the world but the quietest'.

By 1929, the Underground was carrying over six million passengers each year, creating an unprecedented effect on London's environs. Dormitory suburbs appeared wherever there was a tube line. Between 1924 and 1926, the Northern Line reached north to Edgware and south to Morden. The Watford branch of the Metropolitan Line opened in 1925 and electrification was extended from Harrow-on-the-Hill to Rickmansworth.

Regular tube maps were published, with clear timetables advising passengers they could travel from 4 a.m. until 1 a.m. the following day. Places to visit were advertised – concert halls, shopping areas, museums and theatres, all aimed at the more affluent traveller. By the late 1920s, commuters could purchase a first-class three-month season ticket on the Metropolitan Line from Rayners Lane to Liverpool Street for approximately £6, or £4 for a third-class seat.

By contrast, overground rail transport was less well-organised. In 1920, a hundred steam rail companies carried freight, mail and passengers countrywide. It was an inefficient nineteenth-century system; the perpetual soot was blamed for damaging lungs and blackening buildings. Increasing road competition for both freight and passengers forced the rail companies to amalgamate into four major networks in 1923.

Some showcase trains glamorised rail travel, including two famous express trains, the *Royal Scot*, and the *Flying Scotsman*, the latter's namesake locomotive shown at the 1924 British Empire Exhibition. Despite investment, modernisation and electrification, none of the railway companies made a healthy profit.

For the more adventurous, air travel offered an alternative. Airships remained popular. A 1928 advert for the R100 and R101 in *The Illustrated London News*, described 'hotel'-style accommodation for a hundred passengers. However, airships soon declined after the tragedy of the R101 crash in 1930, when forty-eight passengers and crew perished, including air minister Lord Thomson, a personal friend of the prime minister, Ramsay MacDonald.

The future was the aeroplane. Regular international commercial flights between London and Paris began in 1919; by 1924 about thirty-five thousand passengers had flown with British air companies. State backing was given to Imperial Airways, later British Airways, who planned to run scheduled flights, not only to Europe, but across the British Empire; by 1929 they had reached India.

However, it was many years before long journeys were routinely undertaken by air. Most long-distance journeys were by sea. Steam ships carried goods, mail and passengers – in class-differentiated accommodation. For the wealthy, there were cruises on luxury liners run by influential companies such as P&O, Cunard and some newer shipping lines, giving a renewed boost to sea travel.

Above:
London Underground maps were first produced in 1863. With regular changes and updates, they became the model for railway maps worldwide. This 1926 map is printed on stiff linen-backed tri-folded card, the first of eleven editions of Underground maps designed by Fred H. Stingemore in the inter-war years.

Left:
Boarding the Cunard Liner RMS *Franconia*, Liverpool Dock, 1923. Cruising in the inter-war years became popular as an 'up market' holiday. Britain, France, Germany, the Netherlands and Italy all competed for customers.

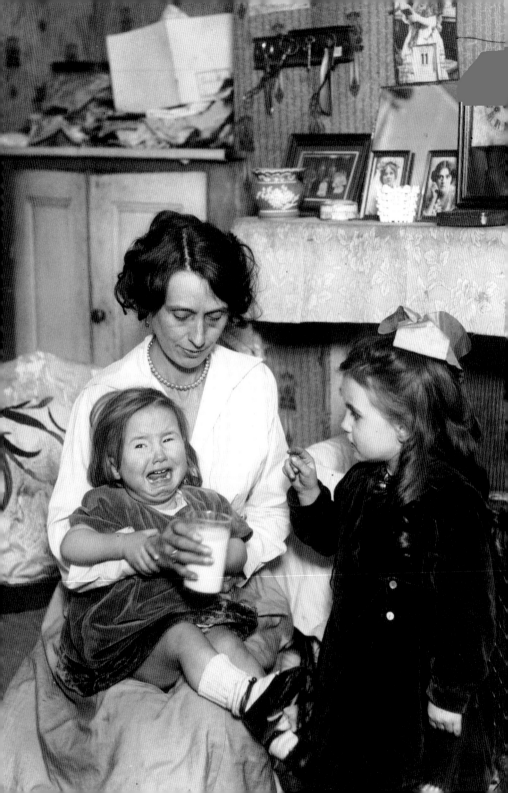

FAMILY LIFE

IN 1920, twelve-year-old Queenie Powell, having won a scholarship to Cyfarthfa Castle Grammar School, Merthyr Tydfil, South Wales, tried to complete her homework while looking after her step-siblings. Most families expected older girls to take a major role in caring for younger children. In *Cider With Rosie*, Laurie Lee recalled his early life dominated by his sisters – feeding him, clothing him, scolding him, hugging him.

In general, there was far less contact between parents and children in the 1920s than later in the century when a more child-centred approach was prevalent. Adults of all social classes frequently delegated child care, or expected children to fend for themselves. Wealthier families, with an eye on their social calendar, employed nannies and governesses, or sent children away to boarding school. Many working-class children were expected to help in the home. They learned to be self-sufficient, usually playing outside all day with minimal supervision.

The role models for many parents were Albert, Duke of York, later George VI, and Elizabeth, who married in 1923. Instantly popular, they symbolised stability and a new start after the war years, cemented by the birth of their daughters, Elizabeth in 1926 and Margaret in 1930.

The smaller size of the new Royal family also typified the late 1920s. A decline in the birth rate across all classes was evident by the end of the decade, mainly due to a better knowledge of birth control. Large families such as Sam Shepherd's and Violet Chapman's, each with ten children, became less common, replaced by families averaging fewer than four children. Smaller families generally meant a better standard of living.

The concept of childhood as a distinct stage, together with new ideas about child psychology, became fashionable in the 1920s, as evidenced in journals like *Parents' Magazine*. The younger generation was gradually becoming a more identifiable group with, for example,

Opposite: Post-war parenting, c. 1920: note the nutritious drink of milk and the family bric-a-brack.

An only child, Ivy Warren has a fashionable cloche hat and dolls' pram at 12 Parr Street, Hoxton, east London, c. 1929. Ivy was Sam Shepherd's niece, the daughter of Rose (née Shepherd) and Bill Warren.

specifically designed children's clothing appearing in the shops. Pocket money became more common in the 1920s; some middle-class children received 3d a week; working-class children, if they received anything at all, about a halfpenny.

Yet there was still an abiding belief that children needed old-fashioned control and discipline. The methods of child expert Dr Frederic Truby King, author of the bestseller *Mothercare Manual*, who advocated a firm regime – such as not 'spoiling' the child with too much attention, strict potty training and suppression of thumb-sucking – remained influential, if controversial, from the twenties until after the Second World War.

When the Duke and Duchess of York toured Australia in 1927, they left eight-month-old Elizabeth at home and had no communication with her for six months. On their return to London the princess did not recognise them. Children whose parents were based abroad, notably in India, often did not see their parents for years.

In many instances, parental control extended beyond childhood. Working-class parents had a major say in their children's futures, especially as, after the school-leaving age of fourteen, children frequently became essential contributors to a family's financial income. It was generally accepted that working-class children would follow their parents' occupations, with, for example, new generations going automatically into the mills or down the pits.

Even before the war, the church had started to play a less central role in family life. There were hopes within the religious community that the war would reunite nation and church, but this did not happen. Widespread scepticism followed the enormous loss of life in the war years. This trend, together with the growth of consumerism, distanced many people from the church. Dissatisfaction with conventional religion led to a growth of minority cults, such as spiritualism with grieving families seeking to contact their war dead.

While the synagogue was still relevant for many Jewish families, declining church attendances afflicted the Church of England, the Catholic Church and particularly the Free Churches. The consecration of war memorials, followed by annual memorial services, was often the only visible sign of community church involvement. The Church of England still performed baptisms, weddings and burials, but little else; church pronouncements on birth control were increasingly ignored.

However, youth movements, centred around established religion and imperialism, such as Boy Scouts, Girl Guides and the Boys' Brigade, were popular with parents concerned about loss of parental control in a time of uncertainty. Youth dances organised by churches were seen as far more acceptable than commercial dance halls. Sunday Schools still attracted large numbers, if only because good attendance meant permission to go on the prized annual Sunday School outing, usually to the seaside. For working-class children this was often their only holiday.

Pacifist youth movements, such as Kindred of the Kibbo Kift (1920) and its offshoot the Woodcraft Folk (1925), were popular with a minority. With an anti-capitalist and anti-militaristic approach to scouting, they were the antithesis to the dominant church- and empire-based youth culture.

Links between the established churches and other associated organisations, such as Dr Barnardo's and The Salvation Army, led to scandalous social engineering in the 1920s. A 'mixture of misguided philanthropy and blatant imperialism', redolent of the nineteenth century, led to children from

The Barnes family, from Woolwich, on a day-trip to London's nearest holiday resort, Southend, c. 1921. Elizabeth Barnes, wearing a hat, is the mother of Fred, Doris, George and Dick (twins). The children's aunt has accompanied her to help with the children. Note the brand-new metal buckets for the children to play with on the beach.

poor homes, orphanages and Poor Law institutions being compulsorily and permanently sent to the British dominions of Canada and Australia. Although some charitable groups believed they were saving children from destitution, many were erroneously told their parents were dead or had abandoned them. Very few checks were made on the children's welfare once they had been deported.

Despite the falling birth rate, numerous poor families struggled in the 1920s on meagre incomes in overcrowded living conditions. Although in many working-class areas there was a strong sense of community – e.g. front doors were never locked – privacy was virtually non-existent in houses with multiple occupants. Accommodation was so cramped that much time was spent outside the home. Children played in the street, women socialised at communal front doors. Many men frequented pubs where women were still mostly unwelcome.

Poverty often led to debt, such as unpaid doctors' bills. Overdue rent, leading to eviction, was the ultimate catastrophe. With nowhere else to go, people turned to pawnbrokers or moneylenders. In Liverpool in 1924 there were 1,380 moneylenders, charging extortionate rates of interest of between 400 and 800 per cent.

There were attempts by churches and charitable institutions to alleviate some of the worst extremes of poverty. The Brighton, Hove and Preston Blanket Lending Society lent blankets to poor families during the winter months. A deposit of ten pennies secured three

Five children on a doorstep in the predominantly Chinese working-class Pennyfields district of London's East End, c. 1928. The children look clean and well-fed. All appear to be wearing shoes and socks – a sign that their families were at least coping week to week.

blankets, repayable if the blankets were washed before return. However, only recipients recommended by middle-class subscribers to the scheme were eligible.

Some families were fortunate to receive help from relatives. When Ernest Seeley's father died in 1920, his three unmarried aunts helped support the family.

Many soldiers returning after the war soon became husbands and fathers, seeking a better life for their new families. It was often hard to leave the war behind. R. Dudley Pendered and his wife Adele, a Voluntary Aid Detachment (VAD) nurse, married in the 1920s. They were both badly affected by their experiences. Richard was wounded and Adele had lost a brother and a fiancé in the same week.

With the advent of the car, seaside places and spa towns became fashionable as family holiday destinations throughout the 1920s. According to *Eve* magazine in 1920, towns such as Bath, Bournemouth, Cheltenham and Torquay were not only popular with families but with large numbers of 'elderly spinsters' holidaying alone.

Elderly single women did not cause concern – unlike the large number of young single women unable to find husbands. A high number of men who died in the war were unmarried; a generation of potential husbands had been lost. National census figures for 1921 revealed approximately one million seven hundred and fifty thousand more women than men across England and Wales. Stories about the

'Uncles': Blackmore, Benjamin & Sons pawnbroker's shop on the corner of Poplar High Street in London's East End, c. 1925. Items not redeemed – probably within a period of twelve months and one week – were put up for sale. Blackmore's windows were full of unclaimed items – note the paintings, instruments, tableware and stacked cases in the doorway. Cheaper items, like everyday clothing, would be further back inside the shop.

Territorial Army officer, Captain R. Dudley Pendered, convalescing after the First World War. Many soldiers wore their uniforms on special occasions after the war was over.

'two million who can never become wives' and 'Our Surplus Girls' made almost daily newspaper headlines for many months.

Even with advances in equality after the war, unmarried women were held in low esteem, as 'desexed and masculinised'. The view of Charlotte Haldane, wife of the eminent scientist J. B. S. Haldane, that single women were genetically inferior was not unusual. Despite a paucity of men and increased employment opportunities, the dominant view persisted that marriage should be a woman's goal and that women's war work had blinded them to their *raison d'être* – to be wives and mothers. Women's magazines were full of advice on how to keep husbands happy and children well cared for.

In January 1929, *Good Housekeeping* reiterated that marriage remained 'the best job for a girl'.

For those middle-class women who did find husbands, living in the newly built suburbs was not always ideal. Young couples were often miles away from their relations and wives frequently spent long hours alone. The continuing emphasis on domesticity discouraged work outside the home.

The 1920s witnessed an increase in family breakdowns. The divorce rate was five times higher than before 1914. There were small signs of some growing equality between the sexes. The first female jurors appeared in divorce courts in 1921, and the 1923 Matrimonial Causes Act made adultery by either partner sufficient reason for divorce. Women no longer had to prove desertion or cruelty, resulting in an increase in divorce petitions by wives. In the upper echelons, prejudices still survived; divorced people were excluded from Ascot's Royal Enclosure and from the Honours List. However, although the Roman Catholic Church continued to categorically oppose divorce, the Church of England began to accept its inevitability by the end of the twenties.

While divorces were abhorred, or at least regretted, weddings were celebrated. Even if the family income was limited, maximum efforts were made to 'put on a good show'. When Sam Shepherd's eldest sister, Rose, married Bill Warren in 1926, all the family were invited. With nine siblings, partners and children, this meant a large gathering for the traditional photo – with the tiered wedding cake taking pride of place.

Rose Shepherd and Bill Warren's wedding photograph, taken in the back yard of 12 Parr Street, Hoxton, east London, 4 April 1926. The yard was not large and it must have taken some time to get everyone into position. Shepherd family: Sam (white shirt), top row; brother Ted (white shirt), left, front row; older brother Alfred, standing second row, third from right. Their mother, Rose, middle row, third from left; their father, Alfred, right foreground, with dog.

Magnet

HOUSEHOLD
ELECTRIC APPLIANCES
MADE IN ENGLAND

Labour Saving

HOME AND NEIGHBOURHOOD

ONE OF THE MAIN ISSUES facing Britain at the start of the twenties was a huge shortage of adequate housing, particularly for poorer families. It was estimated that lack of building during the war years had left a deficit of about eight hundred thousand homes.

In many industrial cities and towns, where numerous properties were unfit for human habitation, working-class families frequently rented rooms in older Victorian houses. These lacked basic amenities, such as a bathroom, hot water and an inside toilet. The outside lavatory, shared with other families, was usually in the back yard, where children also washed in all weathers under a cold-water tap. Open coal fires, blackening the walls, remained the principal form of heating, and often cooking. Mice, rats and other vermin were commonplace in these sub-standard homes.

Islington, where Vi Chapman and Ernest Seeley grew up, was one of London's most densely inhabited boroughs. It contained a notorious slum in Campbell Road, known as Campbell Bunk. With a reputation for violence, prostitution and a lack of law and order, it was commonly known as 'the worst street in north London'. In the 1920s, most cities had neighbourhoods where crime against people and property was rife. Pickpockets, often in gangs, fleeced passers by, and also worked crowds elsewhere at fairs, racecourses or railway stations. The advent of the motor car in the city led to new-style 'smash-and-grab' raids on jewellery shops. An easy escape was possible – until the police brought in their own fast vehicles by the end of the decade.

Sam Shepherd was born and raised at 12 Parr Street, Hoxton, one of the poorest areas in east London and home to the infamous Nile Street gang of pickpockets. Sam remembered visiting 'Daddy Birts', depicted in A. S. Jasper's well-known *A Hoxton Childhood*. This charity ran a soup kitchen and gave free boots to local barefooted children. Like many inner city areas, Hoxton suffered from bad housing – many furnished rooms were rented by the week, or even by the day.

Opposite: A 'Magnet Household Electric Appliances' advertisement, 1920s. Magnet promoted their electric appliances as the perfect way to ease household drudgery and increase leisure time for families without servants.

A Leeds slum, occupied throughout the 1920s. Of almost four million houses constructed in the inter-war years, only twenty-six thousand were specifically built to relieve overcrowding or to allow slum streets to be demolished.

In Liverpool, families lived in houses that had been condemned as early as the 1850s; Glasgow's slums were notorious. Sometimes a third of a working-class family's income went on rent for a home unfit for human habitation.

Some alleviation of the housing problem came from government intervention, heralding a short-lived housing boom. The 1919 Housing and Town Planning Act made councils directly responsible for finding remedies for local housing needs. Government subsidies initially led to the construction of over two hundred thousand new homes. However, the 1921 slump curtailed progress and nationwide concern over poor housing escalated. Both private enterprise and local authorities built insufficient houses for rental and the building boom mainly benefited the private sector. Many landlords evicted tenants to sell their homes to owner-occupiers or developers who preferred to invest in buildings for sale, rather than rental. A 'House to Let' sign, 'not two miles from the City of London', was so unusual it was featured in *The Daily Herald* in September 1923.

The 1924 Wheatley Housing Act, probably the first Labour government's greatest achievement, increased government subsidies, leading to a further half a million new council houses. Skilled workers benefited most, as the poorest unskilled still could not afford council rents.

Those who did manage to move to new council estates faced different problems. Transport costs increased as estates were frequently some distance from people's work. Facilities were often limited. Queenie Powell's sisters moved to Bristol in the 1920s where not one Bristol housing estate had a cinema, social centre or pub.

Britain in the 1920s was far from a mono-cultural society; different minority groups had arrived over many years from across the globe. In the inter-war period, many immigrants were those fleeing communism and fascism.

By the 1920s, the Irish were the largest immigrant group, with around half a million in mainland Britain, although after the founding of the Irish Free State in 1921, the main migrants were Protestants. The small Chinese community in east Limehouse, Poplar, began in the 1890s, but only numbered around five hundred by the 1920s.

After the war, immigration declined owing to the effects of the aliens restrictions acts of 1914 and 1919. However, small groups of Sikhs and Muslims from the Punjab worked as pedlars and hawkers in different British cities. There was also an established Indian community. Shapurji Saklatvala, a Parsee, was elected as the Labour and Communist MP for Battersea. By the end of the decade, Italians began opening successful small businesses, particularly in London, with cafés, restaurants and ice-cream factories.

However, there was also evidence of racism and discrimination. In the post-war years, there were riots in docklands in Cardiff, London and Liverpool. In the 1920s, the Jewish community in the East End migrated to the new outer suburbs, such as Golders Green, Hendon and Ilford, owing to the London County Council's restrictions on jobs, rented housing and education scholarships.

Local vicar with Chinese shopkeepers outside their grocery shop, Turners Buildings, Pennyfields, London E14, *c*. 1920s. Although few in number, the Chinese in east Limehouse (Poplar) became a distinct community based around the Pennyfields area.

Children at Stepney Jewish Club, 1929. By the start of the First World War, London was probably more cosmopolitan than at any time in its history. The Jewish community brought a strong cultural inheritance with them from Eastern Europe.

It was not only the working classes who had to rent their homes. By 1930, only a fifth of the middle classes were home-owners. Councils often preferred families with regular incomes who were less likely to default. The first tenants on Bristol's Fishponds Estate were mainly teachers, clerks and reporters.

Susan Warren and Bertram Peck's wedding, Sturton Street, Cambridge, c. 1920. Both bride and groom came from large families. Bertram was a mechanic. Susan delivered milk with a horse and cart, worked in a laundry, and also as a cleaner. Note the local tin factory behind the soldier in the back row.

Cambridge, known for its famous university, had its own areas of poorer housing. When Susan Warren and Bertram Peck married (*c.* 1920), they posed for their wedding photograph in the back yard of a house in Sturton Street, south Cambridge, adjacent to a local tin factory. Having the wedding reception, or 'breakfast', at home was common among many working-class families. Most houses in this part of Cambridge were rented but the groom's father, Christopher, at times a warehouse and grocery porter, bought his terraced house in Blossom Street in the 1920s for £300.

Some middle-class families still lived in large pre-war houses, designed to be serviced by domestic help. Post-war, few women wanted to return to domestic service and the number in service fell dramatically. Instead of 'live-in' servants, families in new, smaller, houses often employed 'daily helps', or no help at all. This led to an increase in the production of domestic appliances. Magazines like *Good Housekeeping* increasingly advertised labour-saving devices, such as vacuum cleaners for new middle-class homes with carpets.

For lower-income families, however, these appliances were either inappropriate – most working-class homes had linoleum on the floor, not carpet – or were too expensive to buy or run. The gradual introduction of electricity led to an increase in expenditure as families abandoned cheaper fuels such as gas or coal.

Aspiring middle-class families found one answer to their housing needs in the growth of new suburbs on the outskirts of many cities. In London, the concept of 'Metro-Land' had been conceived and fostered by the Metropolitan Railway Company, which rapidly developed lines out into Middlesex, Hertfordshire and Buckinghamshire.

The 'Metro-Land' revolution: a Metropolitan Railway Company advertisement for homes in the London suburbs, within easy commuting distance from the City, *c.* 1920s. Note the house has been built in the very popular Tudor style.

Advertising leaflets proliferated, promoting attractive new housing, and 'Metro-Land' became a household word. 'Ideal Homes' in Pinner Hill, Surrey, were advertised, optimistically, as only 'twenty minutes from Baker Street' on the Metropolitan Line. Hugh Casson, the architect, later renamed Harrow 'Metro-Land's capital' while John Betjeman, later Poet Laureate, recalled the attractions for Londoners of 'beechy Bucks'.

In 1921, Edgware was a small village in north-west Middlesex. By the end of the decade, after the Northern Line tube extension from Golders Green, it became an accessible London suburb, just thirty-five minutes from the centre, serviced by regular trains. Edgware's population rose dramatically by 1,167 per cent between 1921 and 1939.

Almost all London's suburbs expanded. Builders cut costs by simplifying house construction, lowering prices and appealing to a wider market. Detached and semi-detached properties of a similar design and quality appeared all over the country, with a demand for houses with gardens. Typical houses built in the 1920s were smaller than those built before the war but included internal toilets, bright interior decoration, and in many instances, the telephone became a norm, providing households with instant communications. In the late 1920s, homes near Rayners Lane station on the Metropolitan Line were advertised at £895 for a small semi to £1,350 for a larger detached house. Mock Tudor and cottage styles were popular. London's famous store, Liberty's, adopted a Tudor-style frontage in 1925.

A house in Langdale Road, Hove, Sussex that was built in 1924 (photographed in 2009). It became common for houses to be constructed in pairs, with only small differences in style, and with common driveways leading to garages at the back.

Domestic cooker exhibition, Leeds, 1923. All the products in the exhibition were produced by Tricity – kettles, toasters, irons, water heaters and fires ('with flames like a coal fire at its best'). Cookers could be hired from Leeds Corporation Electricity Department for a quarterly rental of fifteen shillings.

Welwyn Garden City in Hertfordshire, Britain's second garden city after Letchworth, was founded in 1920 to attract people away from the capital. New affordable freehold housing on the coast, like Peacehaven in Sussex, 'a short ride from the Aquarium, Brighton', appealed to middle-class families. Brighton was already a commuter city, just an hour's train trip from London. Many new buildings also began to include garages. Houses in Langdale Road, Hove, built in 1924, had rear garages with a common driveway reflecting the new importance of car ownership.

Housing was prioritised in the annual *Daily Mail* Ideal Home exhibitions. Futuristic designs were very popular. The 1928 exhibition envisaged a house of the future with pneumatic furniture and under-floor heating. A 1923 domestic cooker exhibition in Leeds was more realistic, advertising cookers for rent, not purchase.

There were still many wealthy individuals whose lives fascinated average Britons. Thousands flocked to see Queen Mary's Dolls' House at the 1924 British Empire Exhibition. It attempted to authentically represent state-of-the-art upper-class living – the bathrooms had modern plumbing with flushable toilets and a heating installation produced warm water.

This was of little help to the poor. In 1928, a survey revealed that the slum problem had not improved since 1918; there were still more than two million overcrowded houses.

PARIS

Paris Fashions Number

OCTOBER 15·1927

SHOPPING AND FASHION

FOR MANY, AN OVERALL improving economy and the development of new technologies led to notable changes in shopping habits in 1920s Britain. A distinctive feature was the growth of a mass consumer market, bringing important changes in production and retailing. With an increasing number of households enjoying more disposable income, 'new consumerism' began absorbing a rising share of middle-class family expenditure.

The development of new materials transformed shopping. 'Wondrous new' plastic replicated expensive materials like ebony, amber, or onyx, bringing a touch of luxury into less-wealthy homes. Non-precious costume jewellery became increasingly popular, emphasising appearance rather than cost, such as the synthetic pearls displayed at the 1924 British Empire Exhibition. The increasing availability of home electricity led to the purchase of more electrical items like kettles, toasters, and for some, washing machines, from shops eager to satisfy the latest requirements. The 1920 Ideal Home Exhibition displayed many modern appliances and equipment. Some successful premises, like Edward Collier's hotel in South Wales, diversified, providing both goods and services.

For the very poorest, however, shopping was not about obtaining desirable goods, but having enough money for tomorrow's food. BBC Radio Archives hold moving recordings of women recalling poverty-stricken childhoods in the 1920s – asking the butcher for bones to make soup, or for items to be put 'on the slate' to be paid for, hopefully, the following week. The chances of the poorest families purchasing meat, let alone poultry, were virtually non-existent.

Going to the pawnbroker was commonplace. Precious family treasures like wedding rings, Sunday best clothing or even bedding would be hocked and frequently never redeemed. Pawnbrokers' tickets from Clay Cross, a Derbyshire mining community, in the 1920s record items of basic clothing – boots, skirts, trousers, shirts and blouses.

Opposite:
Vogue magazine adopts an up-to-date Art Deco-style front cover, 15 October 1927. Although it had been running for many years, *Vogue* became a far more successful up-market magazine in the 1920s when it began to feature the latest women's fashions.

Unaffordable for many: ducks, geese, chickens and rabbits for sale at a poultry stall, 1928. Although there was an increased demand for eggs by the start of the 1920s, only the better off bought poultry for home consumption. Rabbit was a much more popular meat for lower-income families. The poorest could rarely afford any meat at all.

Sam Shepherd remembered his mother's regular weekly trips to 'Uncle' to obtain a pittance for essential food and household necessities.

Better-off working families began to obtain cars and radios through hire purchase. Furniture industry profits nearly doubled between 1924 and 1934 as buying on the 'never-never' became popular. However, there was always a strong chance of losing products through payment default; slipping back into poverty was an ever-present danger.

Consumerism was at the heart of the huge 1924 British Empire Exhibition, staged to promote the economic value of the British Empire. Held in rural Wembley, 7 miles from the centre of London

A multi-purpose establishment: Central Temperance Hotel, Pentre, Rhondda, South Wales, Easter 1928. Looking like a shop, Edward Collier's premises actually comprised a hotel, a bakery, a shop and a restaurant, plus a large upstairs room for dancing. Note the signs for 'dinners', 'teas', 'restaurant', and 'hot cross buns'. Edward was a Master Baker and Confectioner. He kept his business going throughout the 1920s but by 1932 was badly affected by the depression and had to file for bankruptcy.

but accessible by two new railway lines, it gave the suburbs an enormous boost. George V, who opened the exhibition with the first-ever royal radio broadcast heard by seven million listeners, sent himself a celebratory telegram transmitted around the world in eighty seconds. The exhibition was a massive affair, visited by ten million people. Specially hired buses brought schoolchildren from east London. London Underground advertisements urged visitors to travel by tube for 2/9d return, including admission. The public admired the large stadium, built a year earlier for the 1923 FA Cup Final. Queen Mary's Dolls' House, a Chinese restaurant, an Indian pavilion, the new *Flying Scotsman* locomotive and a recreation of Tutankhamun's tomb were popular exhibits; Ernest Seeley travelled by tube especially to see the 'palace of engineering'. Much was built in the new modern medium, concrete. Well-attended, the exhibition re-opened for a further six months in 1925 but eventually made a financial loss; the cost of staging it was just too great.

Safety First!: a children's game from the late 1920s, reflecting the mounting topical interest in cars and road safety. Toy manufacturers were quick to recognise the profitability of linking their products to adults' interests as well as children's.

Afterwards, 'British made' or 'Empire made' labels became synonymous with patriotism and quality. 'British cars for British folk', urged a 1925 advertisement in *The Illustrated London News* to persuade customers away from cheaper American vehicles. Aggressive American-style advertising was increasingly adopted; as early as 1920 British brewers produced branded beer mats.

It was not only the adult consumer market that expanded. A rapid post-war recovery by the British toy industry brought a wider range of toys into the shops. 'It isn't patriotic to buy foreign-made toys' remonstrated a 1923 advertisement in *The Times*. Dolls appeared in the latest fashions, doll's houses reflected contemporary architecture. Deans, a top British manufacturer, produced the popular toy dog, Dismal Desmond, mascot both for the England cricket team and Wimbledon's ladies' changing rooms.

Meccano Ltd became Britain's largest toy company, producing both Meccano, available in nine different kits by the 1920s, and from 1925, the first clockwork Hornby train sets. Trains, planes, ships and cars were among the most successful toys, reflecting the growing adult passion for travel, as did topical games and kits such as *The Young Wireless Operator*, *Greyhound Racing* and *Wembley*, 'the British Empire Game'. For those who could not afford dearer items, there were cheap inflammable celluloid toys that could be replaced for a few pence. Hamleys became the world's largest toyshop and the rebuilding of Regent Street by 1927 gave a boost to all forms of shopping in the capital.

Across the country, household names such as Woolworths wooed new consumers. Marks & Spencer recognised the profitable field of cheap women's clothing, producing rayon as well as cotton garments. Home & Colonial Stores expanded prominently in the south, as did the family firm, Sainsbury's, who focussed on the burgeoning middle classes, doubling their shops in the inter-war years, while United Dairies controlled most of London's milk trade. The Co-op, with its generous dividend (share of the profits based on purchases), was popular in working class areas, especially in the industrial north. Everyone knew their Co-op 'divi' number; Vi Chapman's number was 147919. Ernest Seeley banked there, Vi and Sam Shepherd shopped at London stores; all three were later buried by the Co-op.

Between 1920 and 1939, British ice-cream consumption grew expeditiously. Walls introduced 'Stop Me And Buy One' tricycles but it was Lyons, adopting American mass-production techniques, that was dominant, gaining an exclusive contract with Odeon cinemas by 1930. Independent ice-cream sellers still made a living selling from street to street, especially in London.

Alongside the new multiples, many small specialist shops still flourished. People shopped daily at butchers, grocers, greengrocers and fishmongers, and took their own jugs to off-licences to fill with draught beer. London 'Ham and Beef, or 'Cooked Meat' shops roasted huge sides of beef, pork and game, with unsold meat turned into rissoles, pies and sausages. Encouraged by the rapid expansion of large meat importers such as Union Cold Storage, butchers increasingly installed refrigerators. Shop hygiene improved; by the late 1920s, cellophane was increasingly used to cover food. Some items were still individually cut, weighed and wrapped but many small grocers started to purchase packaged supplies from wholesalers.

Street sellers, especially in London, increased throughout the 1920s. In rural areas, travelling salesmen were still common. Dry Drayton in

Independent ice-cream vendor, Grundy Street, London's East End, c. 1929–30. In central London, a popular Italian ice-cream seller, Mr Allocca, was a familiar sight in 1921 with his patriotically decorated ice-cream cart, with images of King George V and Queen Mary on the side.

Cambridgeshire was virtually self-sufficient, visited by a butcher, baker, grocer, hardware salesman, knife-grinder and French onion seller. Local farms provided milk and honey; vegetables and fruit were grown in cottage gardens.

Following Howard Carter's 1922 discovery of Tutankhamun's tomb, all things Egyptian became fashionable – ornaments, clothes, handbags, hairstyles and headgear. This Egyptian craze coincided with the start of Art Deco, the 'moderne' decorative style immensely popular in the inter-war years. With bright colours, straight lines, geometric patterns, exotic influences and an emphasis on streamlining, Art Deco styling was evident in clothing, sculpture, furniture, household items, transport and buildings, such as London's redesigned Oxo building. When the Art Deco Carreras building opened in north London in 1928 it was both the largest cigarette factory and largest reinforced concrete building in the world. Gradually, Art Deco was reproduced cheaply for the masses. Clarice Cliff's pottery with colourful angular designs was hugely successful; Queenie Seeley treasured one surviving plate all her life.

Above:
A street seller with three puppies for sale at Club Row, one of London's well-known East End street markets, near Petticoat Lane, 1925. Club Row was famous for its pet market, 'teeming with dogs and birds'.

Left:
High-street shopping in the 1920s. Note the fashionable cloche hats, strap shoes and shorter skirts. Cheaper copies of expensive upper-class styles were becoming available for the mass market.

Learning the *Tutankhamen Shimmy*', 1920s. The shimmy was a popular dance for 'flappers' in the 1920s. An Egyptian craze swept Britain after Howard Carter's discovery of Tutankhamun's tomb in 1922 received worldwide press coverage.

The 1920s witnessed more liberated styles of clothing, particularly for women. Reluctance to relinquish their wartime independence extended to fashion. New choices favoured straight, masculine lines; curves were out. Dress lengths shortened; waistlines dropped to the hips. 'Artificial silks' – rayon decorated with printed patterns – became all the rage. Women's underwear was lighter and easier to wear; sales of corsets declined by two-thirds. Buttons and complicated lacing were out; zip- and snap-fasteners were in.

London was the centre of men's fashion, although styles changed less radically. Ex-servicemen still sometimes wore their pre-war

Men's fashion did not change as radically as women's. Hats were the one essential. Left to right: Mr Roote (bowler); Mr Kefford (trilby); 'Gordon' (flat cap); Mr Bass (trilby). Great Yarmouth promenade, 1926.

clothes and wealthier men did not change their clothes as frequently as their Edwardian forebears. Visiting American students brought the influential 'Oxford bags' trousers to Britain in the mid-twenties.

Hats remained important for both sexes with numerous advertisements – 'Four hats for ten shillings' urged the cheaper newspapers. Neat cloche hats became popular for all women, worn with the new, short, bobbed hairstyle. Men's headgear was generally more class based, a top hat or Homburg for the wealthy, fedora or trilby for the middle classes, flat caps for the working man.

In *The Glass of Fashion* (1954), society fashion photographer and costume designer Cecil Beaton described typical wealthy upper-class girls from 1926: 'short tubular dresses, cigarettes in long holders, cloche hat, bobbed hair, plucked eyebrows, bands of diamond bracelets from wrist to elbow and earrings hanging like fuchsias'. They were frequently referred to as 'flappers', following the latest dance fashions emanating from America. Their style was soon eagerly copied by girls from other social groups.

Some of Beaton's fashion trendsetters belonged to the Mayfair set known as the 'Bright Young Things'. Stephen Fry adopted this title for his 2003 film of novelist Evelyn Waugh's brilliant, sophisticated 1930 satire, *Vile Bodies*. It depicted a decadent, wealthy, post-war generation, with no serious thought for the future, seeking to distance itself from the aftermath of war.

"Always fill your "Caddy" with E & S C.W.S. TEA

FOOD AND DRINK

THE FIRST WORLD WAR left an important legacy in terms of food and health. Over a third of conscripts, mainly working class, had been declared physically unfit for military service during the war. Government rationing and price controls of basic foods had to some extent improved people's diets during the war and raised national standards of health. By spring 1921, controls were abolished, but better health became as important for the British people in the twenties as improvements in housing.

In inter-war Britain, the quality and provision of food generally improved with demand. Per capita consumption of essential foods, such as eggs, butter, margarine, fruit and vegetables increased in comparison with earlier years. Post-war Britain returned to a free trade economy with much of its food imported, particularly from the Empire. Ten to fifteen ships arrived daily at London docks and other British ports, bringing wheat from Canada, Australia and Argentina; refrigerated New Zealand lamb and butter; and bacon and eggs from Denmark.

However, domestic suppliers suffered. British farming, sustained by government subsidies, had expanded during the war, but afterwards had to face renewed overseas competition, either by becoming more efficient, or by concentrating on the foods with which they could best compete, notably dairy and market garden produce.

At the start of the decade, there was little food regulation. Bread, in particular, especially from small suppliers, was poor; the ratio of flour to water varied widely and unexpected 'extras' were often discovered. In *Cider With Rosie*, Laurie Lee listed the different things his family found in their loaves – 'string, nails, paper and once a mouse'. Following improvements in food processing and distribution, this situation gradually improved, especially in towns, with the growth of three large companies dominating the bread market, Rank, Spiller and the Co-op. Local suppliers, however, were often badly affected.

Opposite: Co-operative Wholesale Society (CWS) advertisement for tea, 1920s. An unusual advertisement, it shows a cup of tea being given to a golf caddie. The Co-op was most successful among working-class areas of Britain, particularly in the north, where golf was unlikely to have been the sport of choice. Note: the advert is making a pun on tea 'caddy' and golf 'caddie'.

Wide variations in real wages (income measured against changes in prices), and fluctuations in employment, hid marked inequalities in diet and health between different social classes and regions in Britain, most noticeably between the industrial north and the more affluent south.

Poorer families were still compelled to eat very frugally. Much of their diet comprised carbohydrates – potatoes, poor-quality white bread and sugared tea. Betty Stevenson, remembering her Glasgow childhood for the BBC, recalled a diet of boiled onions and scotch broth made from a bone, sometimes given to them by the butcher.

Laurie Lee described eating mostly vegetables in his Gloucestershire village; there was little money for meat. This was not uncommon in rural areas where meat was often only bought for Sunday and had to last all week.

With a better understanding of the connection between food and good health, middle-class consumers began to seek not only better quality food, but a wider range and regularity of supply. This increased demand led to many well-known brands appearing in the twenties, like Shredded Wheat – '100 per cent food yet costs only 8d for the biggest packet'. Lyons began selling their vacuum-packed coffee and Smiths, only later including its distinctive blue paper twist of salt, brought crisps to the masses. In 1928 over a million packets were sold across Britain.

With the end of sugar rationing in 1920, Tate & Lyle virtually monopolised Britain's huge demand for sugar, for sweets, jam, and millions of cups of tea; Cadbury's Creme Eggs first appeared in 1923. Sugar was also added to a new breakfast food, cornflakes, reaching Britain from America in 1924; producer Kellogg hired unemployed

It's the modern way: buying Blue Band margarine over the telephone, late 1920s. There was increased competition between the manufacturers of butter and margarine by the 1920s. Margarine was marketed as a similar-quality product available at a cheaper price.

"Never mind the butter then—

I would rather have BLUE BAND.

I can always rely on it."

BLUE BAND
MARGARINE
" Just like *best* Butter "
—but only 1/- per lb.

men to give away free samples. The abundance of sugar led to a growth in the demand for cakes; women's magazines like *Good Housekeeping*, and the cheaper *Wife and Home*, increasingly featured new recipes.

Canned food was extremely popular in the inter-war years; Heinz and Crosse & Blackwell began to dominate the market. Tinned peas, pilchards and pears were cheap and convenient staple foods, with, as a treat, tinned peaches. Tinned fruit was eaten by both middle and working classes but fresh fruit was less popular and usually eaten stewed. The exception was the banana, with one million imported annually in 1900, rising to eleven million by 1924.

A typical home meal for many middle-income families might include sausages or steak and kidney pudding, boiled potatoes, peas or cabbage and apple pie or jam sponge with custard to follow. Roast lamb or beef with Yorkshire puddings was often eaten on Sundays.

Britain's favourite food, fish and chips, reached a peak of popularity during the inter-war period. Harry Ramsden opened his first shop near Leeds in 1928; by then, the National Federation of Fish Friers estimated there were 30,000–35,000 fish and chip shops across the country.

Above: Smiths corners the market: A late 1920s Smiths crisps advertisement linking its product to the increasing middle-class passion for picnics on days out with the car.

Left: A packed Thames nightclub restaurant in Twickenham, 1925. Nightclubs with restaurants were popular among the well-to-do. Note the champagne bottles, women in hats and waiters with bow-ties.

Until the advent of cheaper restaurants, eating meals out was mainly only enjoyed by the better-off. However, Lyons Corner House restaurants started to be successful in the twenties, drawing customers from different social backgrounds. In 1928, a new Lyons on the corner of Oxford Street and Tottenham Court Road produced twenty-one-thousand meals on its first day, served by waitresses in black and white uniforms, later known as 'Nippies'. Menu prices were varied, to appeal to a range of incomes, from soup at five pence to lobster mayonnaise at two shillings and sixpence. Good-quality London restaurants began to provide a better standard of cuisine to the aspiring middle classes at 3s–5s per head. The first kosher Bloom's restaurant opened in London's Brick Lane in 1920.

The opulence of the Edwardian era disappeared after the war, although the wealthy could still eat extravagantly at places like the Ritz,

No piped water. Uriah Harper, who lived by the Methodist chapel in the village of Dry Drayton, Cambridgeshire, carries buckets of water on a yoke from the village pump in 1929. This cottage was one of a group of buildings known as 'Spike's Huddle' in Pook Lane, later demolished. The couple by the gate are Mr and Mrs Fitches.

Bottled water for the affluent: an advertisement for Malvern Bottled Water, 1920s. Malvern Water was first bottled in the 1850s. From 1927 it was piped from a spring about 2 miles from Malvern and bottled at the local Colwall family factory.

Savoy and Carlton. At home, the upper classes began to eat only three or four courses per meal; at the wedding of the Duke and Duchess of York in 1923 there were only eight courses, half the number that would have been served twenty years earlier. Differences between food eaten by the upper and middle classes became less noticeable.

By the inter-war years, the quality of water in most areas had greatly improved as it became regarded as an essential public utility. In many rural areas, however, water often still had to be collected in buckets from shared village pumps.

Tap water was considered safe to drink although water was mostly used to make tea. Advertisements urged the better-off to purchase bottled spring water from places like Malvern.

The consumption of tea grew during the 1920s, reaching a peak at the height of the Depression, 1929 to 1932, when prices were low and tea duty was abolished. Tea generally remained far more popular than coffee, even though the retail price of both drinks was similar. Queenie Powell's father was a grocer in South Wales, and colour-blind. As tea was packaged in several different-coloured packets according to quality, in order to distinguish between them, he would number the packets.

Tea consumption improved sales of fresh milk, although it was still too expensive for many families and there were also concerns about quality. Poorer families usually bought canned condensed milk.

Tea on the rocks: bathers enjoy a cup of tea on the beach at Plymouth, Devon, 1921. Tea was regarded as Britain's unofficial national drink. One of the most successful brands was Lyons, who not only sold packets of tea but served numerous 'cuppas' in their famous Lyons Tea Shops.

Cheaper than the pub. *The Happy Go Lucky* off-licence, owned by brewers Mann, Crossman and Paulin, Strattondale Street, Cubitt Town, in the East End,1927. Crossman and Paulin amalgamated in the nineteenth century to establish a brewery at Isleworth, which later became Mann, Crossman and Paulin.

It lasted longer in the days before home refrigerators, was sweetened with sugar and regarded as safer. From 1922, all fresh milk was pasteurised to prevent the spread of tuberculosis but it was some time before habits changed. Ernest Seeley's mother, Agnes, fearing contamination, never drank fresh milk, only tinned. In an attempt to increase sales, the National Milk Publicity Council, established in 1922, adopted the slogan 'Drink More Milk' and it gradually became seen as a healthy food, especially for children. Scottish children taking part in a 1925 experiment were given a daily pint of milk; their general health improved and their growth rate increased by approximately twenty per cent.

National Milk Publicity Campaign Week: students at St Ignatious Catholic School receive a lecture on nutrition, 9 July 1925. The National Milk Publicity Council was founded in 1920 and successfully provided information about milk nutrition, and promoted the consumption of milk, cream and English cheese. Sales of milk soared in the 1920s.

During the war there were severe alcohol restrictions and by the start of the 1920s there was a significant drop in consumption. Stricter licensing laws, a small tax increase and restricted pub opening hours accounted partly for lower consumption, but the main reason was a change in attitudes and behaviour after the war. Drinking habits changed. Younger people spent more time in dance halls and cinemas than pubs, although there were gradually more women in pubs than before the war, reflecting their new-found independence. Beer consumption, particularly, remained at a fairly low level during the 1920s. The 1921 Licensing Act retained afternoon pub closure and limited opening hours to eight a day, or nine in London. Many street corners had off-licences selling alcohol at a cheaper rate than the pubs.

Family circumstances also played a significant part. Ernest Seeley, who had an alcoholic grandfather, became and remained, teetotal. Sam Shepherd's father was notorious for his drinking, seriously affecting his family's income and livelihood in the inter-war years.

The high duty on spirits meant only the better-off could afford to purchase them. Enduring images of 1920s 'bright young things' imbibing cocktails are representative of only a very small percentage of the population. High prices also limited the sales of soft drinks during the twenties, similarly seen as luxury items.

With more disposable income, plus advances in the production and distribution of food, a healthier, more varied diet was enjoyed by many people by the end of the decade; but the financial crisis that came in 1929 heralded a new era of depression.

Overleaf: Tea Room with a view: a 'Nippy' waitress serves afternoon tea at a Lyons Corner House, 1920s. Note the density and variety of transport, old and new, in the traffic jam outside.

HEALTH

A FTER the post-war global influenza epidemic that killed forty million, 1920s Britain witnessed gradual but sporadic improvements in general health. Standards were still dependent on social class, income, employment status and geographical location. The Ministry of Health, established in 1919 with Dr Christopher Addison, medical doctor, politician and ardent social reformer as its first minister, was given wide-ranging responsibilities for public health, housing, the Poor Law, hospitals and infirmaries.

In the twenties, affluent Londoners were attracted to 'Metro-Land', where 'the good air of the Chilterns invites to health by the day and to sleep by night'. Middle England was acquiring an interest in healthy living, evident from magazines such as *Open Air* 'for lovers of Nature and Outdoor Life', or for a minority, the leading naturist magazine, *Health and Efficiency*.

This was in stark contrast to deprived east and south London where working-class Bermondsey, renowned for its public health department and pioneering welfare services, was the exception. Some thought Bermondsey's coat of arms should display a healthy child in a green field with the motto 'It can be done'.

Before the advent of the National Health Service, there were distinct differences in the quality of medical attention that different social classes could receive. The 1924 Labour government advocated improvements in health care but their proposals proved too costly. Health insurance benefits increased, but there were no major administrative changes in the 1920s. The 1911 National Insurance Act still applied. Insured workers, if they fell ill, received some income, together with free drugs and basic appliances from 'panel' doctors who participated in the insurance scheme. However, their families, like the uninsured, had no such entitlement.

Those paying for medicines often incurred debts that took years to settle. Others paid a few pence weekly to friendly societies to cover

Opposite:
Infant Welfare
Exhibition
advertisement,
Battersea Town
Hall, c. 1925.
Battersea was
one of a number
of London
boroughs
promoting infant
welfare in the
1920s.

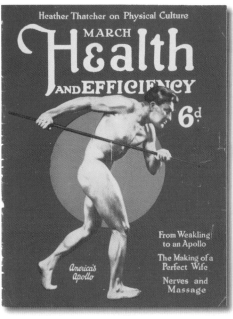

Above: Promoting healthy living: *Health and Efficiency* naturist magazine. Founded in 1900, this March 1927 issue had a feature on how to achieve a healthier body but also, with an emphasis on domesticity and relationships, an article on being the perfect wife.

Above right: 'Perfect Prescription Service': Boots advertisement, 1920s. Boots was established in 1849. By the 1920s, there were six hundred branches across Britain.

medical bills. Some could afford reputable chemists, such as Boots, others went to local 'druggists', who dispensed pills and potions for any number of conditions.

Woolworths sold over-the-counter spectacles for those unable to afford eye tests and dental decay was rife. Many illnesses went unreported. The last resort was the dreaded Poor Law; in 1929, Poor Law medical services were transferred to local authorities but facilities often remained inadequate.

Far fewer children died in epidemics after the war than before but most childhood memoirs from this period mention at least one illness. A Wiltshire school logbook records school closures for a variety of different illnesses in the 1920s. Laurie Lee's first year was plagued by 'diphtheria, whooping cough, pleurisy, double pneumonia and congestion of the bleeding lungs'. He was not expected to survive. Many illnesses were linked to chest complaints. Although decreasing, tuberculosis had not been eradicated. Ernest Seeley's father and two aunts all died of tuberculosis in London in the 1920s.

Poor sanitation aggravated the problems. In the poorest areas good hygiene was almost impossible. Many children who died before their first birthday suffered from diarrhoea caused by poor hygiene and inadequate nutrition. While the middle classes might choose between different soaps, some poorer families were still using old insanitary earth closets (toilets).

Wealthier classes often had minimal understanding of the poorer classes' struggle to maintain good hygeine. 'I do not blame the working man because he stinks, but stink he does', wrote W. Somerset Maugham condescendingly in 1922.

Forward-looking councils promoted better sanitation. A 1923 Leeds Public Health exhibition offered to help people convert their trough water closets into 'modern sanitary conveniences'.

In poor families, mothers were frequently ill-nourished, voluntarily the last in line for food. Maternity benefit was still low.

C.W.S
GREEN OLIVE SOAP
for Beauty & Health

'Use soap for Health and Beauty': 1920s CWS advertisement for Green Olive Soap. The Co-op was attempting to gain a foothold in the wealthier consumer market.

A 'National' nurse exercising with a group of children, 4 June 1929, as part of the work of the National Council for Maternity and Child Welfare, established in the 1920s to promote the welfare of mothers and young children.

Rickets, from a poor diet and lack of vitamin D, affected a woman's bones; a misshapen pelvis could result in difficult, painful births. While other death rates improved, maternal mortality did not. In poorer areas, the main reason was malnutrition. Among the middle classes, maternal mortality actually increased from the mid-1920s, probably from infected doctors' instruments causing fatal puerperal fever.

Important new services, such as day nurseries, health visitors and child welfare clinics, followed the Maternal and Child Welfare Act (1918), but as the act was voluntary, take-up varied. Where intensive maternal and child welfare intervention was introduced, there were noticeable improvements.

Health-conscious London boroughs included not only pioneering Bermondsey, but Kensington, where young children 'at risk' received routine checks. Woolwich was one of the few boroughs in the country to provide pre-school units and Battersea also promoted infant welfare. The North Islington Infant Welfare Centre began in 1913 with nine mothers; by 1920 numbers had substantially increased.

School medicals, introduced before the war, raised concerns over the health of children from the increasing number of unemployed families. In addition, school meals varied in quality and quantity, often least nutritious in areas of highest unemployment. More free school meals were provided in Nottingham than before the war but less was spent per head, resulting in cheap meals such as hash or potato pie that were high in carbohydrates, but low in protein.

Illness was feared, for both financial and medical reasons, resulting in a common dread of hospitals. Those who could afford to pay found their money could not guarantee a good result. Although improving, the hospital system was uncoordinated. Where there was increased government aid, as with the establishment of maternity hospitals, provision improved. Where aid was limited, notably for the mentally handicapped, provision was poor, with many patients remaining in Poor Law institutions.

Many hospitals were run by private voluntary trusts, providing twenty-five per cent of all hospital beds. Patients were means-tested, any other finance came from donations. As voluntary hospitals mainly treated the poor, this caused financial difficulties; new equipment and salary increases often exceeded donations. In the early 1920s, A. J. Cronin was a doctor at Tredegar Park Cottage Hospital in Wales.

Operating theatre: three surgeons and a nurse, all gowned, pose with an anxious young patient awaiting an operation, still with a bow in her hair. Westminster Hospital, May 1921.

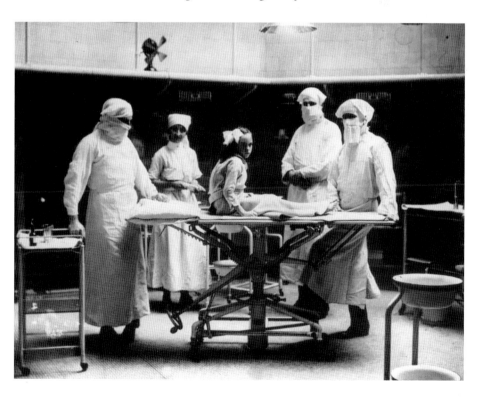

Open-air nursing: child, Joan Green (centre), recuperating after hospitalisation for rickets, Oxford, 1925. Rickets is a softening of the bones in young children, leading to fractures and deformity. It is primarily caused by poor diet, notably a lack of vitamin D and calcium.

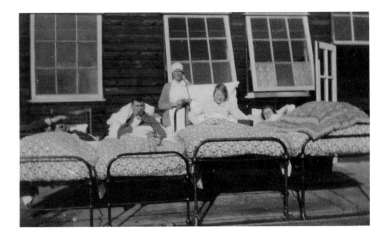

In his novel, *The Citadel* (1937), Cronin criticised both the health care provided by such hospitals and doctors' training. A shortage of young doctors – many had died in the war – only exacerbated the situation.

Despite improvements in medical expertise and the development of new drugs, criticisms of medical care were well-founded. Operations were dangerous, recovery slow. Infections spread quickly. Although penicillin was 'rediscovered' by Alexander Fleming in 1928, it was many years before antibiotics were in regular use. In some instances, 'routine' operations, such as the removal of tonsils, were performed at a patient's home; the cost was lower and the fear of hospitalisation, if not of infection, removed.

The dire financial plight of the East End's large London Hospital reached Parliament in June 1920. There was only sufficient money to settle the hospital's bills for eight weeks. The government agreed to match donations for The London and other insolvent hospitals, and, by the mid-twenties, problems eased.

Standards of nursing could vary in crowded East End hospitals. Patients were often referred to by numbers, had unwashed hair and were allowed visitors only twice weekly. However, by the early 1920s, nursing was striving to be recognised as a profession, rather than just a 'caring' job. Apart from mental health nurses, who were routinely undervalued and badly paid, all nurses were compulsorily registered and trained from 1920, with state examinations from 1925.

Open-air nursing was still common in some hospitals. London's Great Ormond Hospital sent children to a Surrey convalescent home where sliding glass doors allowed in fresh air, seen as beneficial to those suffering from tuberculosis or rickets.

With scant public awareness of the health dangers, smoking reached a height in the inter-war years. Hollywood films glamorised the habit and an increasing number of 'newly liberated' women smoked in public. Collectable cards tucked inside cigarette packets encouraged consumers to smoke even more.

Only ten per cent of a doctor's patients were private, yet they often provided half a surgery's income, demonstrating the vast gulf between rich and poor. Wealthy patients were often prepared to try experimental treatments. Psychoanalysis became fashionable, although viewed by mainstream doctors as risky and untried. The development of child psychology, with a growing awareness of mental as well as physical needs, led to American-style Child Guidance clinics opening in the mid-1920s. Behaviourist methods, training children through reward and punishment, also became popular.

One of the major political issues in the inter-war years was birth control, termed a 'health' issue by Labour politicians fearful of losing the Catholic vote. Before 1929, it was illegal for welfare centres to provide contraceptive advice as the state was not prepared to fund the provision of free birth control information. Help was only available, at a cost, from private doctors. Abortions among working-class women were still very common, easier to access than contraception.

Women wanted more control of their lives, and most critically, their bodies. In London, Dorothy Lansbury, later Mayor of Shoreditch, was prominent in an increasingly vocal birth control movement, demanding universal access to free information. The huge impact of birth control campaigner, Marie Stopes, was noticeable early in the decade when she founded the Society for Constructive Birth Control. From 1921, her Holloway clinic offered the first-ever free service to married women. Stopes was a fanatical eugenicist, promoting contraception to eliminate what she regarded as 'low grade' reproduction, but her actions gave hope to ordinary families overburdened with numerous children.

Birth control led to a dramatic and fundamental change in family size. Pre-war, few couples practised birth control; post-war it was the majority, although contraceptives were still regarded with distaste by many and Boots refused to stock them. Before the war, twenty-five per cent of married women had over five children. Thirty years later the average family size was almost down to two. This birth rate decline was noticeable across all classes. Fewer babies meant better provision could be made for existing children. The growing use of contraception, plus improvements in living standards, meant many families could live more comfortable lives than their parents.

SCHOOLS AND PENSIONS

FOR THE YOUNG, educational opportunity in the 1920s was still largely determined by birth. A large, free, state elementary sector catered mainly for the working class. Many middle-class children went to fee-paying independent preparatory and grammar schools, while the privileged upper classes attended more expensive, mainly residential, public schools.

Most children received schooling in free elementary schools. Many were 'all age', providing a basic education for children in either mixed, or single-sex, schools. Typically, an elementary school child attended school from age five to the school leaving age of fourteen, and then went straight into employment. Victorian half-time schooling for factory children officially ended around 1922, although it was slow to die out in industrial Lancashire. The main emphasis in elementary schools in the twenties was still on reading, writing, arithmetic and religion. Older boys were often taught drawing and there was a continuing emphasis on basic housework skills and needlework for girls. Other subjects such as history, geography, science and music were also included. Enterprising schools tried to widen their pupils' horizons. Children at a Wiltshire elementary school took part in local folk-dancing days and in 1927 recorded songs for a Columbia Records Company competition.

Most inter-war memoirs recall rote learning and corporal punishment. 'Twice two are four. One God is Love. One Lord is King. One King is George. One George is Fifth ...' recalled Laurie Lee in *Cider With Rosie*. His teacher, nicknamed Crabby, was always armed with a ruler, ready to knock 'some poor boy sideways'. There were also the dreaded school inspections – the brief 1928 report for Dry Drayton village school in Cambridgeshire noted 'steady progress, orderly conduct and diligent industry'. Elementary leaving reports, 'characters', were brief; in 1925, Vi Chapman at fourteen was described simply as 'honest, punctual and trustworthy'. She kept her 'character' for the rest of her life.

Opposite: Celebrating Empire Day: pupils at Hugh Middleton schools, Clerkenwell, 1928. Note the pet bulldog in the foreground. Other Empire Days in the 1920s were recalled by a Streatham schoolgirl later in life – 'on 24 May ... we would march around the playground ... waving the Union Jack, singing *Land of our Birth*. There was also a very popular half-day holiday.'

Standard VIa girls' class (approximately 11–12 years old), at Wilmont Street Elementary School in London's East End, 1926. The 1918 Education Act had raised the school-leaving age from twelve to fourteen.

The monotony of the elementary curriculum was brightened by festivals such as Empire Day, when many children wore scout and guide uniforms or sported patriotic colours; or occasional trips out of school, as when Poplar schools assembled for a swimming gala. Children from all over the country travelled to the British Empire Exhibition in 1924. Time off was given for religious festivals such as Ash Wednesday and Ascension Day.

Despite growing evidence of the need for nursery education, the welfare of children under five had a very low priority. Some attention

A London schoolteacher instructs his students how to protect their eyes while watching the solar eclipse, 24 June 1927. The elementary curriculum was widening and more opportunities were taken to introduce children to different learning experiences.

was given to the specific needs of five- to seven-year-olds but in overcrowded areas large classes of around sixty pupils frequently made this difficult. High numbers in London schools were a huge drain on the London County Council's resources, accounting in 1924 for nearly half its annual expenditure. Learning by rote was often the only practical teaching method when many city schools had classes of over forty. Rural schools tended to be smaller; throughout the 1920s, the roll at Dry Drayton rarely exceeded forty-five.

The number of elementary schoolchildren peaked in the late 1920s and there was a corresponding increase in the number of teachers entering the profession. Most teacher training colleges were large authoritarian institutions, particularly for young women. Arriving at Hereford Training College in 1929, Queenie Powell complained to her family about oppressive rules and regulations restricting individual freedom.

Women teachers, who dominated the elementary sector, were particularly undervalued at the start of the decade. In 1921, fifteen per cent were married but for a while, to cut costs, many local authorities refused to appoint married women and those in post were often dismissed on marriage.

Occasional days out of school also broadened the curriculum, such as this swimming gala held at Poplar Baths, East India Dock Road during the 1920s. Special display days were sometimes introduced when schools were open for visits from the local community.

However, schooling was improving. A wider, better-resourced curriculum was advocated by the Board of Education in *A Handbook of Suggestions for Teachers* (1927), and in professional journals like *Teachers' World*, which began publishing its famous educational journal *Pictorial Education* the same year.

Most concern in the 1920s centred on education for children over twelve. It was evident from the poor condition of war recruits that Britain's economy would not become more competitive without an educated workforce. Only a small percentage of elementary pupils passed the scholarship to gain a free grammar school place and even fewer accepted the offer. Although tuition was free, the uniform, books and other extras, were not. Furthermore, many families could not afford the loss of a child's potential earnings, which often kept them above the poverty line.

In 1926, The Hadow Report, *Secondary Education for All*, examined the education of the 'adolescent'. Its title became a slogan for the future. Hadow recommended raising the school-leaving age to fifteen, and made a clear demarcation at eleven between primary and secondary levels. It was the most important inter-war educational measure, which paved the way for the major 1944 Education Act.

During the twenties, demands for secondary schooling increased and standards slowly improved. Those children fortunate enough to be in grammar schools began to take new school certificates that provided a standardised benchmark for employers, but candidates had to pass in five subjects to obtain 'matriculation'. Queenie Powell described 'getting matric' as extremely traumatic; one failed exam meant all five had to be retaken. The curriculum was still mainly arts-based. Despite industrial advances by Germany and America, Britain responded slowly to the urgent need for better scientific and technological training. By 1929, more children were moving from elementary schools into free secondary schools but the odds against were still thirteen to one.

The most disadvantaged group of all, pauper children, still attended schools run by local Poor Law authorities – in London, some were large residential 'District' institutions dating from the Victorian era. Music was an area in which pauper boys were encouraged to train, in preparation for future employment as bandsmen in the armed forces. District schools like Shenfield Training School in Essex, where the Poplar Guardians sent their children, established successful bands.

None of the resourcing problems that mired the education of the poorer classes affected the children of the wealthy. The annual fee at

Children of the Shenfield Poor Law Training School Band, Essex, proudly parading through their home borough of Poplar. Shenfield band played outside Brixton Prison when George Lansbury and fellow councillors were imprisoned (Poplar Rates Revolt, 1921).

Evan Sheriff James pushing his wife Isabella to the park in Alken Street, New Town, Wigan, where they would often spend the day talking to unemployed ex-servicemen.

Eton was £210 during the 1920s, more than a skilled worker's annual earnings. Girls at prestigious fee-paying secondary schools like Roedean were given an academic education and prepared for careers outside the home, in direct contrast to girls from the elementary sector.

Most public school pupils went on to Oxbridge or other established universities. University entrance tended to be narrow and elitist because of the high costs involved. Where parents could afford the fees, places could usually be found. Only one and a half per cent of those aged eighteen to twenty attended universities in the year 1919–20, lower than in any other European country.

Working-class children rarely obtained university places. Ernest Seeley, the eldest of three children, was an exception in securing a place at Imperial College, London. Subsidised by his mother's cleaning job, plus money from his three aunts, he eventually achieved a Ph.D. In 1929, he was appointed 'Teacher of Chemistry' at Bournemouth Municipal Technical College, during a marked expansion in the number of technical colleges. By contrast, his youngest brother, Stanley, although equally bright, left school at fourteen with no qualifications. Later becoming a conscientious objector in the Second World War, in the twenties he tramped the streets, playing his violin and frequently staying overnight in workhouses.

At the other end of life, an increasing number, approximately six per cent of the British population, two-and-a-half million people, were aged over sixty-five at the start of the 1920s. Of these, a million, mainly women, were over seventy. Many were vulnerable, infirm and in dire financial straits. Improving their situation presented a severe challenge.

At the start of the century, the sole recourse for elderly people in need was to the Poor Law but this became increasingly morally unacceptable. In 1908, a means-tested non-contributory pension, introduced by Asquith's Liberal government, gave those over seventy years of age five shillings per week, doubling in 1919 to ten shillings. Any income above that was gradually offset against the pension.

During the early twenties, as their pensions increased, pensioners theoretically had more disposable income; pensions were up one hundred per cent, and retail prices down seventy per cent. Yet a 1923 survey estimated that a married couple on full pensions needed over two shillings a week more just to buy the 'necessaries of life'; a single pensioner needed a further three shillings to acheive even the most basic standard of living. By the mid-1920s, the number receiving a pension reached nearly one million.

In 1925, the Widows', Orphans' and Old Age contributory Pensions introduced contributory pensions. Integrated with national health insurance, these new pensions were not means-tested, but financed by contributions from employer and employee, as well as a state subsidy. At sixty-five, insured workers received pensions of ten shillings per week, with dependants entitled to death benefits. A widow received ten shillings per week, with five shillings for the first child and three shillings for each other child. In 1929, the age at which widows received pensions was reduced to sixty. However, economic hardship was not alleviated. Pensioners often had no other resources. In the 1920s, many were ineligible under the contributory scheme; women often failed to qualify even though they greatly outnumbered men. Also, the non-contributory pensions remained second-class benefits.

Ernest Seeley's father died of tuberculosis in 1920. His widow, Agnes, received no widow's pension for five years until 1925 when she received ten shillings per week. Chamberlain's scheme lasted until after the Second World War, establishing the principle of insurance as an integral part of Britain's social policy.

The most important social survey of the inter-war years, the *New Survey of London Life and Labour*, which examined poverty in the capital between 1929 and 1931, revealed that, despite many problems, compared with earlier generations, quality of life for the elderly was improving. Fewer were dependent on their families. Many tried, preferred, and were able, to live independently. Pensions were replacing Poor Law and charity dependency. Self-sufficiency and self-respect in old age was beginning to emerge, albeit slowly.

The Radio Times, December 21, 1923

THE CHRISTMAS NUMBER
RADIO TIMES

6D.

"JUST A SONG AT TWILIGHT"

Registered at the G.P.O. as a Newspaper

Vol. I.—No. 13.

RELAXATION AND ENTERTAINMENT

ENTERTAINMENT in its various forms was a welcome escape and diversion for all classes in a time of mixed fortunes. The rapid development of the annual holiday after the war led to unprecedented growth in resorts like Eastbourne, Hastings, Blackpool, Bournemouth and Brighton. New forms of transport brought thousands of day-trippers from the towns to the countryside and seaside.

Leisure also changed with the advent of radio. In 1922, the British Broadcasting Company was founded (becoming the British Broadcasting Corporation in 1927). Expensive radio licences cost ten shillings each but over one million were issued by 1925. The first radios had rechargeable batteries ('accumulators') but amateur enthusiasts built elementary crystal sets ('cat's whiskers') using magazines, such as *Popular Wireless* and *Wireless World*. News bulletins began in 1922, weather forecasts in 1923. The weekly *Radio Times* sold on Fridays for two pence. Music programmes became popular, especially dance music and American jazz. 'Children's Hour' was also a big favourite.

At home, alongside the radio, reading was a popular activity. Books were expensive and most people borrowed from libraries. Boots (the Chemist) had a large circulation. Ernest Seeley was an early enthusiastic Boots library member. In the 1920s fiction, especially murder mysteries, was popular. Some crime-writers became household names, notably Agatha Christie. Eminent historians G. D. H. and Margaret Cole wrote detective fiction as a 'sideline' – *Poison in the Suburb* (1929) seemed most appropriate for the 'Metro-Land' era. A range of newspapers catered for a mass readership and sales of magazines soared. Reading materials for children also proliferated: Enid Blyton began her phenomenally successful career in the twenties; *Rupert Bear* was first published in the *Daily Express* (1920) in an attempt to outsell its rivals. Virtually all 1920s children's literature was directed at a middle-class readership.

Opposite: Families gathered round the radio to listen: The first Christmas issue of the *Radio Times*, 21 December, 1923. The *Radio Times* was first issued on 28 September 1923 after newspapers, fearing the competition of broadcasting, refused to carry listings of BBC radio programmes. By 1925, the BBC had gained sole editorial control of the well-known publication.

Day-trippers at the seaside, c. 1929. Despite being on the beach, everyone is fully dressed, the men in jackets and ties, the women in fashionable cloche hats and stockings.

Spend a day in the country: a late-1920s Ordnance Survey one-inch map for Maidstone and Tunbridge Wells, made out of linen and costing three shillings. Note the quiet idyllic scene, and walker with map and pipe, all designed to persuade people out of the towns into the countryside.

ORDNANCE SURVEY
"ONE-INCH" MAP

MAIDSTONE and
TUNBRIDGE WELLS
Mounted on Linen
Price Three Shillings

Dance and music played a significant role in post-war culture as wartime restrictions came to end. The American influence on British culture escalated in the 'roaring twenties' with the arrival of jazz. Palais, Mecca and Locarno dance halls mushroomed, attracting young people of all classes. In London, nightclubs flourished and daytime tea dances were held at expensive hotels. Lyons Corner House in Coventry Street had an orchestra on each floor.

The fox trot, tango, stomp, and later the notorious Black Bottom dance were all popular, but were dwarfed by the Charleston, arriving from America in 1925. With a skilful mixture of loose limbs and tapping feet, Charleston 'flappers' moved their arms like birds as they danced. Band-leader Victor Sylvester taught the Charleston while dancer Santos Casini famously gave demonstrations on the roof of a moving London taxi. 'Doing the Charleston' became an iconic twenties image.

The other popular mass entertainment, and the principal challenge to music and dance, was the cinema, bringing excitement, glamour and escapism. Historian A. J. P. Taylor called cinema 'the essential social habit of the age'. The British film industry was small and poorly funded and films shown in Britain in the twenties overwhelmingly came from the brash new

The first *Rupert Bear* book, written by Mary Tourtel and published in 1924. Rupert made his first appearance in the *Daily Express* newspaper on 8 November 1920. Early Rupert stories fitted well into the 'magical world' that characterised many 1920s children's books.

town of Hollywood. British audiences, notably young women, flocked to see American silent classics like Charlie Chaplin's *The Gold Rush* (1925), *Ben-Hur* (1925) and westerns starring Tom Mix. English-born Stan Laurel and American Oliver Hardy teamed up in 1927 and were among the few artists to make a successful transition from silent films to 'talkies'. Italian film star, Rudolph Valentino, became an international celebrity. His death, at the age of thirty-one, caused mass hysteria among film fans in 1926.

The rapid success of film led to small, mainly working-class, cinema halls, disparagingly termed 'flea pits', being replaced by new magnificent 'picture-palaces'. By 1925, approximately three and a half thousand such cinemas, influenced by the exotic Art Deco movement, tried to replicate Hollywood screen glamour across Britain. The local press called Brighton's sumptuous Regent, with seating for three thousand, a 'Gorgeous Temple of the Silent Drama'. The landmark arrival of the first 'talkie' in 1927, with Al Jolson in *The Jazz Singer*, soon followed.

London's West End was at the heart of British theatre. Noel Coward had four West End shows running simultaneously in 1927. Many thought 1920s British theatre too lightweight, suffering from

"In dancing the Black Bottom - don't let your right hip know what your left hip's doing!"

Dance was everything: Black Bottom cartoon, 1925. Although it originated much earlier, the Black Bottom dance was featured in the Harlem show *Dinah* in New York in 1924.

'undesirable' American influences and dominated by musicals. Yet audiences travelling in from the suburbs, some with 'matinee seats in the pit for half a crown', could watch acclaimed British talent, such as Gertrude Lawrence and Edith Evans. There were new works by J. M. Barrie and George Bernard Shaw. Shaw's play, *Saint Joan* (1923), contributed to his 1925 Nobel Literature prize. The part of Joan was written for the redoubtable left-wing actress, Sybil Thorndike, who supported the General Strike even when it closed the production. By 1925, actress, singer and comedienne Gracie Fields was already a household name. Other popular twenties actresses included, 'English Rose' Gladys Cooper, who, in addition to film and theatre roles, was one of only two women to run a London theatre (the Playhouse) in the inter-war years.

Sport played a significant part in British life and that of the British Empire in the twenties as the British elite took their sports with them to the colonies. At home, people were now participants, spectators and consumers. Sport helped shape identities of gender, social class, local communities and the nation. Particularly popular were gate-money sports, including football (soccer and rugby), cricket, lawn tennis, boxing, greyhound racing, horseracing and golf. Sport offered spectacle, drama and, for many, the opportunity to 'have a flutter'.

Watching sport became relatively affordable for a largely male clientele. *Metroland*, the Metropolitan Line's annual advertising booklet highlighted how convenient the tube was for reaching Lord's cricket ground, 'all the football grounds of London' and 'the principal Greyhound Race-courses'.

'Going to the dogs' became a new national pastime enjoyed mainly by working men, often at evening meetings, including betting on-course with 'bookies' or 'the tote'. By 1927, the new Manchester Belle Vue Stadium attracted seventy-thousand weekly visitors. Forty more tracks opened, with London's famous White City Stadium adapted for dog racing.

Sport for the middle and upper classes also enjoyed a post-war boom. In London's expanding new suburbs, tennis clubs became an important part of the surburban social scene while golf provided opportunities to mix business and recreation. In 1922, the amateur Wimbledon championships transferred to a new stadium, with seating doubled to fifteen thousand as spectators watched the talented young French champion Suzanne Lenglen whose unconventional playing and emancipated dress style epitomised newly liberated 1920s women. Cricket flourished at Lord's and the Oval grounds, but there were still class distinctions between 'gentlemen' and 'players'.

It was during the 1920s that Britain's national game, association football or soccer, played extensively in streets and back yards, developed into a mass spectator sport. In *The Good Companions* (1929), J. B. Priestley captured forever soccer's quintessential appeal for the 1920s working man:

> It turned you into a member of the community, all brothers together for an hour and a half … you [had] escaped from the clanking machinery of this lesser life, from work, wages, rent, doles, sick pay, insurance cards, nagging wives, ailing children, bad bosses, idle workmen, but you had escaped with most of your mates …'

Football's footprint was still on Scottish and northern industrial cities and towns but with a growing challenge from southern clubs. The first

'Having a flutter': on-course bookmaker, Birmingham, 1 November 1926. Betting was at its peak in the inter-war years. The amount spent on all forms of gambling, with horse racing the most popular, rose from £63 million in 1920 to £221 million by 1938.

Arsenal v Preston North End, First Division match (Preston in white), Arsenal stadium, Highbury, north London, 1922. Arsenal defeated Preston North End 1-0. Football became the most popular mass spectator sport in the 1920s.

modern football manager was Herbert Chapman at Arsenal, in north London. From his 1925 appointment until his untimely death in 1934, Chapman transformed football into mass entertainment. Two of Vi Chapman's brothers, Frank and Pat, regularly travelled to watch Arsenal's matches after work in the City.

During the twenties, English rugby flourished internationally whereas rugby in South Wales suffered badly from the economic downturn. Clubs closed as the Welsh deserted the valleys. More policemen than miners in Welsh rugby sides reflected community tensions. Professional Rugby League, so called from 1922, originated in northern working-class towns. In 1929, thousands of fans headed south for the first time when the first Rugby League Challenge Cup Final was held at Wembley.

Young women, enjoying increased independence, became more visible in several sports in the 1920s, with women's football flourishing as a new spectacle. The fame of Dick, Kerr Ladies, with their star player, Lily Parr, endured throughout the twenties. On Boxing Day 1920, an immense crowd of fifty-five thousand saw Dick, Kerr Ladies defeat St Helens Ladies on Everton's ground of Goodison Park. However, in 1921 the Football Association (FA) declared soccer 'quite unsuitable for females' and dealt it a mortal blow by banning women's matches on Football League grounds. Its revival had to wait until much later in the century.

Perhaps surprisingly, it was the recreational game of darts that became the major organised leisure activity in the 1920s. The National Darts Association, established in 1924, led to improvements in venues as brewers upgraded their pubs to meet the challenge of the cinema and the dance halls. Darts competitions were given a high profile in national newspapers. By 1939, as many working men played darts as watched football.

Particularly symbolic in the 1920s was the hosting of the famous 'White Horse' FA Cup Final in 1923 at the new Wembley Stadium. Nearly twice the stadium's capacity of 100,000 spectators arrived en masse, swarming onto the pitch. Not until the arrival of the police, notably PC Scorey on his white horse, Billy, was order seemingly restored. George V was present to see Bolton Wanderers defeat West Ham United 2-0. Royalty always attended FA Cup finals after 1923 and from 1927, 'Abide With Me' was regularly sung before the kick-off. A new tradition of the annual Wembley Stadium FA Cup Final, now famous throughout the world, had been created in the nation's capital.

The Preston Ladies Football Club (formerly Dick, Kerr Ladies) represent England against France in an international match at Herne Hill, south London. English music hall star, George Robey, kicks off, May 1925.

PLACES TO VISIT

Visitors are advised to check opening times before travelling.

13 Mallord Street, Chelsea, London SW3 6DT.
(A. A. Milne's house, can be viewed from outside.)

14 Barton Street, London SE1P 3.
(T. E. Lawrence's home in 1926. Can be viewed from outside.)

17 Dunraven Street, Mayfair, London WIK 7EG. (P. G. Wodehouse lived here from 1927 to 1934. Grade 2 listed. Can be viewed from outside.)

83 Shortlands Road, Shortlands, Bromley, Kent BR2 OJG. (Enid Blyton's home from 1925–9. Blue Plaque. Can be viewed from outside.)

Bethnal Green Museum of Childhood or *Victoria & Albert Museum of Childhood,* Cambridge Heath Rd, London E2 9PA. Tel: 0208 9835200.
Website: www.museumofchildhood.org.uk

The Bramah Museum of Tea and Coffee, 38–40 Southwark Street, London SE1 1UN. Tel: 0207 4035650. Website: www.teaandcoffeemuseum.co.uk

The British Empire and Commonwealth Museum, Clock Tower Road, Temple Meads, Bristol BS1 6QH. Tel: 0117 9254980.
Website: www.empiremuseum.co.uk

Bus Preservation Trust Ltd, Redhill Road, Cobham, Surrey KT11 1EF.
Tel: 01932 868665. Website: www.lbpt.org

The Cenotaph, Parliament Street, Whitehall, London SW1. (War Memorial)

The Cinema Museum, The Master's House, 2 Dugard Way, London SE11 4TH. Tel: 0207 8402200. Website: www.cinemamuseum.org.uk

Clouds Hill, Wareham, Dorset BH20 7NQ. Tel: 01929 405616.
Website: www.nationaltrust.org.uk/cloudshill
(T. E. Lawrence's home, purchased in 1924.)

Durban House Heritage Centre, Mansfield Road, Eastwood, Notts NG16 3D2. Tel: 01733 717353. Website: www.dhlawrenceheritage.org
(D. H. Lawrence's house.)

Gillette Rugby Heritage Centre, The George Hotel, 1 St Georges Square, Huddersfield HDI IJA. Tel: 01484 542458.
Website: www.rlheritage.co.uk (Permanent Rugby League exhibition)

The Jewish Museum, 129–131 Albert Street, London NW1 7NB. Tel: 0207 2841997. Website: www.jewishmuseum.org.uk

London Transport Museum, 39 Wellington Street, London WC2E 7BB.
Tel: 0207 3796344. Website: www.ltmuseum.co.uk

MCC Museum, St John's Wood Road, Grace Gate, London NW8 8QN.
Tel: 0207 6168595. Website: www.lords.org/history/mcc-museum

Museum of British Road Transport, Hales Street, Coventry CV1 1PN.
Tel: 0247 6832425. Website: www.transport-museum.com

Museum of Childhood Memories, 1 Castle Street, Beaumaris, Anglesey, LL58
8AP. Tel: 01248 712498. Website: www.nwi.co.uk

Museum of London, 150 London Wall, London EC2Y 5HN.
Tel: 0207 0019844. Website: www.museumoflondon.org.uk

National Coal Mining Museum, Caphouse Colliery, New Road, Overton,
Wakefield WF4 4RH. Tel: 01924 848806. Website: www.ncm.org.uk

National Football Museum, Sir Tom Finney Way, Preston PR1 6PA.
Tel: 01772 908421. Website: www.nationalfootballmuseum.com

National Horse Racing Museum, 99 High Street, Newmarket, Suffolk CB8
8JH. Tel: 01638 667333. Website: www.nhrm.co.uk

National Motor Cycle Museum, Coventry Road, Bickenhill, Solihull, West
Midlands B92 OEJ. Tel: 01675 443311.
Website: www.nationalmotorcyclemuseum.co.uk

National Motor Museum, John Montagu Building, Beaulieu, Brockenhurst,
Hampshire SO42 7ZN. Tel: 01590 612345. Website: www.beaulieu.co.uk

Pollock's Toy Museum, 1 Scala Street, London W1T 2HL. Tel: 0207 7636
3452. Website: www.pollockstoymuseum.com

Robert Opie Museum, Colville Mews, Lonsdale Road, Notting Hill, London
W11 2AR. Tel: 0207 9080880. (Brands, packaging and advertising)

Rupert Bear Museum, Museum of Canterbury, Stour Street, Canterbury,
Kent CT1 2NR. Tel: 01227 475202.

Shaw's Corner, Ayot St Lawrence, nr Welwyn, Hertfordshire AL6 9BX.
Tel: 01438 829221. Website: www.nationaltrust.org.uk/shawscorner
(Home of George Bernard Shaw.)

Mr Straw's House, 5–7 Blyth Grove, Worksop, Nottinghamshire S81 0JG.
Tel: 01909 482380. Website: www.nationaltrust.org.uk/mrstrawshouse
(A 1920s house captured in time.)

Tenement House, 145 Buccleuch Street, Glasgow, Greater Glasgow & Clyde
Valley, G3 6QN. Tel: 0844 4932197.
Website: www.nts.org.uk/Property/59/Details (Tenement life 1911–61.)

Victoria and Albert Museum, South Kensington, Cromwell Road, London SW7
2RL. Tel: 0207 7942 2000. Website: www.vam.ac.uk (Art and design)

Wellcome Museum, 183, Euston Road, London NW1 2BE. Tel: 0207
6118722. Website: www.wellcomecollection.org (Medical history.)

Wimbledon Lawn Tennis Museum, All England Lawn Tennis & Croquet Club,
Church Road, Wimbledon SW19 5AE. Tel: 0208 946 6131.
Website: www.wimbledon.org

The Workhouse, Southwell, Upton Road, Southwell, Nottinghamshire NG25
OPT. Tel: 01636 817260. www.nationaltrust.org.uk/theworkhouse

World Rugby Museum, Twickenham Rugby Stadium, Rugby Road,
Twickenham TW1 1DZ. Tel: 0208 8928877.
Website: www.rfu.com/microsites/museum/

INDEX

Page numbers in italic refer to illustrations